HOW IT WORKS

THE HUMAN BODY

Text by Kate Barnes

Illustrated by Steve Weston

*To Maurice C. Wat__
From Lauita K Watson
(mom)
I love you always!!.*

HORUS EDITIONS

ISBN 1-899762-27-2

First published 1995
This edition first published 1997
Second impression 1997

Published by Horus Editions Limited,
1st floor, 27 Longford Street,
London NW1 3DZ

Printed in Singapore

HOW IT WORKS
CONTENTS

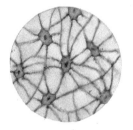

How the Body Works

DO YOU know what lies inside your body and how your body works? The following pages will take you on a voyage of discovery. Along the way you will find out how each system in the body functions and how all the systems work together to make us the complex human beings we are.

In particular, you will see how each part of the body has its own special job to do, how we get the energy to live, and how we defend ourselves from harm. You will also learn about the five senses – vision, hearing, touch, taste, and smell – and how all we think and do is controlled by the brain in communication with our nervous system. This book explains how and why we breathe, how we move, and how we reproduce in order to keep the human race alive.

HANDS ARE COMPLEX BONY STRUCTURES THAT ENABLE US TO CARRY OUT INTRICATE MOVEMENTS

BEHIND THE INTESTINE LIE THE KIDNEYS, WHICH REMOVE WASTE AND PASS IT INTO OUR URINE

OUR SKIN IS A WATERPROOF PROTECTIVE COVERING FOR THE WHOLE BODY

OUR BONY SKELETON PROVIDES A FIRM ATTACHMENT FOR THE BODY'S MUSCLES

WHERE BONES MEET THERE ARE JOINTS, ALLOWING MOVEMENT TO OCCUR

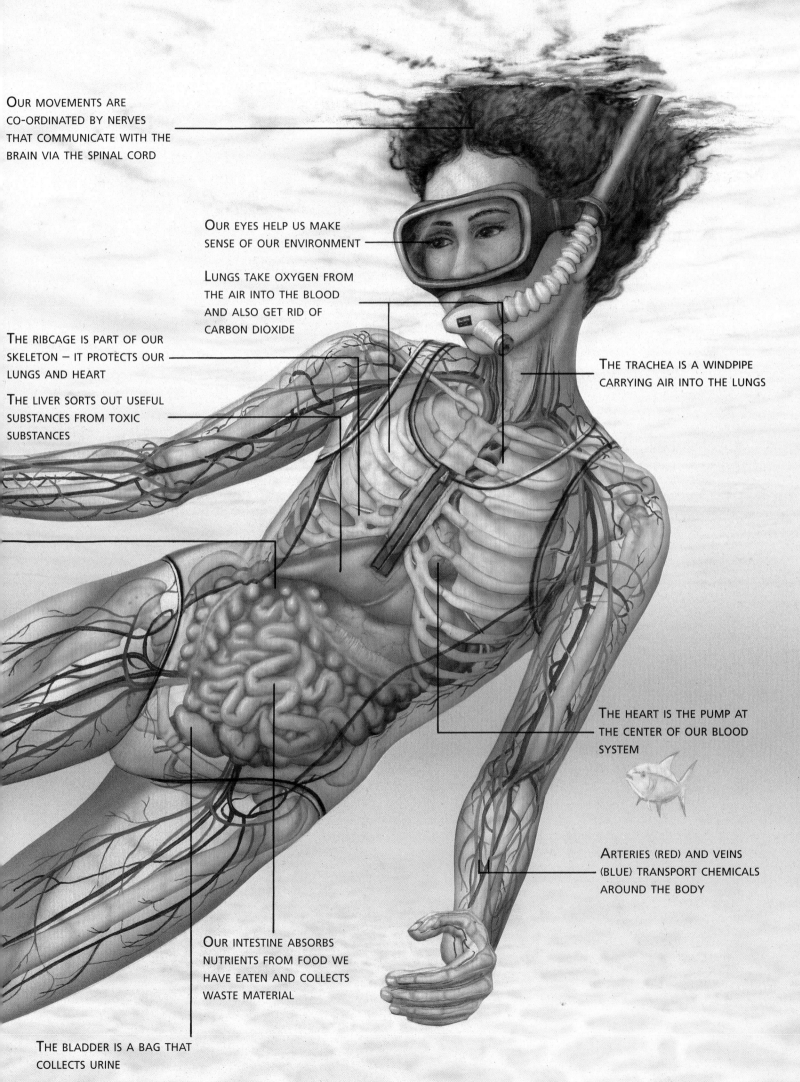

OUR MOVEMENTS ARE CO-ORDINATED BY NERVES THAT COMMUNICATE WITH THE BRAIN VIA THE SPINAL CORD

OUR EYES HELP US MAKE SENSE OF OUR ENVIRONMENT

LUNGS TAKE OXYGEN FROM THE AIR INTO THE BLOOD AND ALSO GET RID OF CARBON DIOXIDE

THE RIBCAGE IS PART OF OUR SKELETON – IT PROTECTS OUR LUNGS AND HEART

THE LIVER SORTS OUT USEFUL SUBSTANCES FROM TOXIC SUBSTANCES

THE TRACHEA IS A WINDPIPE CARRYING AIR INTO THE LUNGS

THE HEART IS THE PUMP AT THE CENTER OF OUR BLOOD SYSTEM

ARTERIES (RED) AND VEINS (BLUE) TRANSPORT CHEMICALS AROUND THE BODY

OUR INTESTINE ABSORBS NUTRIENTS FROM FOOD WE HAVE EATEN AND COLLECTS WASTE MATERIAL

THE BLADDER IS A BAG THAT COLLECTS URINE

Cells

IN TOTAL there are about 50 billion cells in your body! Each cell is so small it cannot be seen with the naked eye. However, with the help of a microscope we are able to study cells and discover how they work.

Nearly all cells have a nucleus, which is the control center of the cell. Ribosomes in cells do as the nucleus tells them. They act like factories, making proteins and other chemicals for our body. To work properly a cell needs energy and this energy comes from the food we eat. Power stations in the cell, called mitochondria, change the energy stored in food into a form of energy that can be used by the cell.

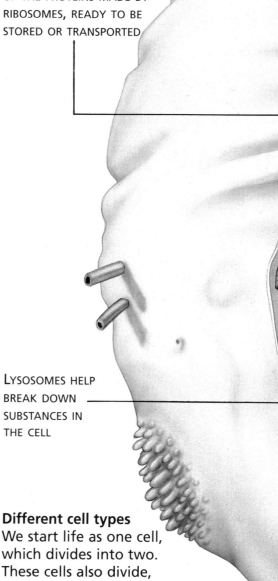

THESE BRANCHING TUBES ARE USED FOR STORAGE AND FOR TRANSPORTING CHEMICALS AROUND THE CELL

THE CELL MEMBRANE ALLOWS FOOD IN THE FORM OF SUGARS TO ENTER, AND ALLOWS WASTE CHEMICALS MADE IN THE CELL TO PASS OUT

THE GOLGI APPARATUS PACKS UP THE PROTEINS MADE BY RIBOSOMES, READY TO BE STORED OR TRANSPORTED

LYSOSOMES HELP BREAK DOWN SUBSTANCES IN THE CELL

BRAIN CELLS

MUSCLE CELLS

LUNG CELLS

BONE CELLS

BLOOD CELLS

Different cell types

We start life as one cell, which divides into two. These cells also divide, and as more cells grow they form different shapes and sizes. Each of these different types of cell has its own job to do. Similar types of cell will join together to make tissues, which form organs like our brain and lungs (*see left*).

How long a cell lives depends upon the type of cell it is. Skin cells die quickly and are constantly replaced by new cells. Nerve cells should last a human lifetime and cannot be replaced even if they are damaged.

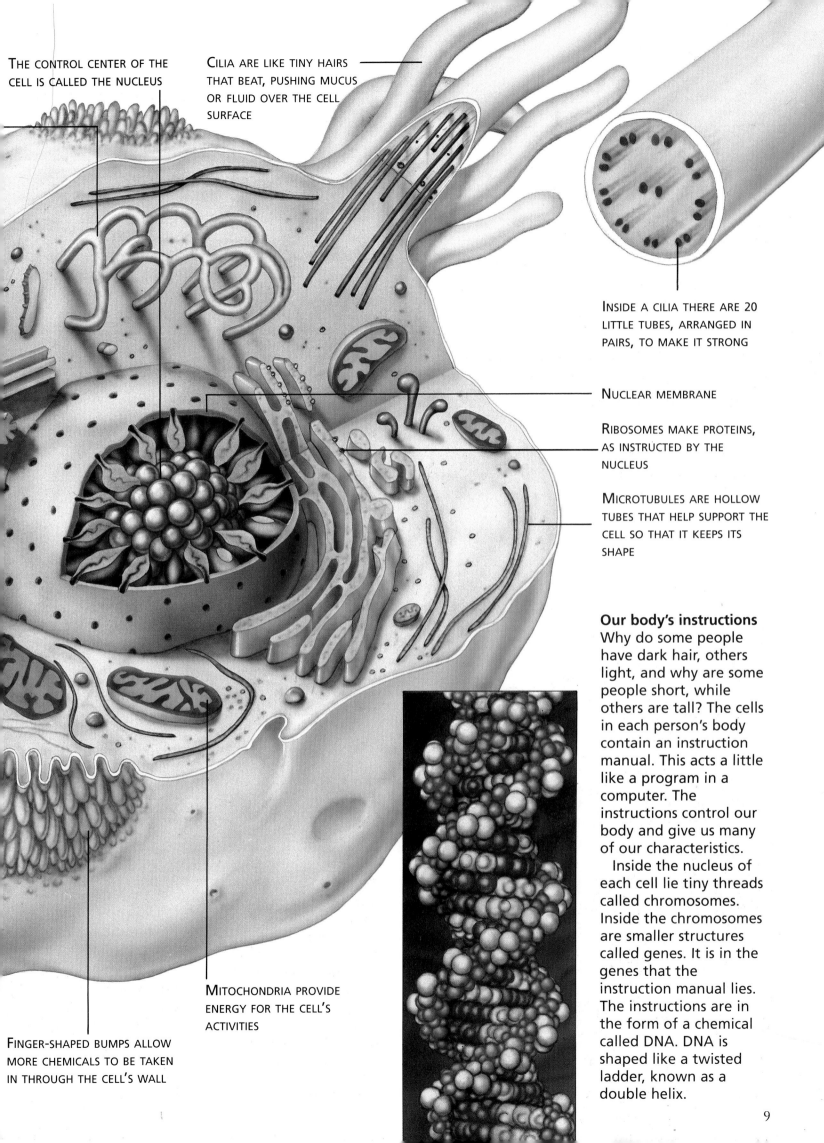

THE CONTROL CENTER OF THE CELL IS CALLED THE NUCLEUS

CILIA ARE LIKE TINY HAIRS THAT BEAT, PUSHING MUCUS OR FLUID OVER THE CELL SURFACE

INSIDE A CILIA THERE ARE 20 LITTLE TUBES, ARRANGED IN PAIRS, TO MAKE IT STRONG

NUCLEAR MEMBRANE

RIBOSOMES MAKE PROTEINS, AS INSTRUCTED BY THE NUCLEUS

MICROTUBULES ARE HOLLOW TUBES THAT HELP SUPPORT THE CELL SO THAT IT KEEPS ITS SHAPE

MITOCHONDRIA PROVIDE ENERGY FOR THE CELL'S ACTIVITIES

FINGER-SHAPED BUMPS ALLOW MORE CHEMICALS TO BE TAKEN IN THROUGH THE CELL'S WALL

Our body's instructions
Why do some people have dark hair, others light, and why are some people short, while others are tall? The cells in each person's body contain an instruction manual. This acts a little like a program in a computer. The instructions control our body and give us many of our characteristics.

Inside the nucleus of each cell lie tiny threads called chromosomes. Inside the chromosomes are smaller structures called genes. It is in the genes that the instruction manual lies. The instructions are in the form of a chemical called DNA. DNA is shaped like a twisted ladder, known as a double helix.

9

The Blood System

OUR BLOOD acts as a transport system, carrying substances around the body. It is rather like a road network, with large arteries as main roads and very small vessels as lanes. Blood itself is made up of a liquid called plasma and two main types of cell – red cells and white cells. Red cells contain a chemical called hemoglobin, which is responsible for carrying oxygen to all the body's cells. White cells are far fewer in number than red cells. Their job is to attack invading germs. There are also small particles in blood called platelets, which help the blood to clot when we cut ourselves.

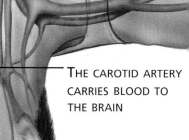

A PERSON'S PULSE IS FELT FROM THE RADIAL ARTERY, NEAR THE SKIN SURFACE

AORTA (MAIN ARTERY)

VENA CAVA (MAIN VEIN)

HEART

BLOOD VESSELS IN THE LUNG

THE CAROTID ARTERY CARRIES BLOOD TO THE BRAIN

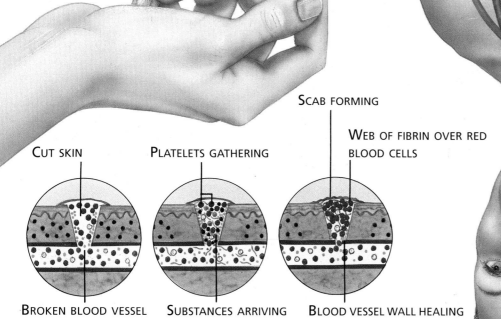

SCAB FORMING

WEB OF FIBRIN OVER RED BLOOD CELLS

CUT SKIN

PLATELETS GATHERING

BROKEN BLOOD VESSEL

SUBSTANCES ARRIVING

BLOOD VESSEL WALL HEALING

Forming a scab

When we cut ourselves, blood vessel walls break. The bleeding stops when enough platelets have stuck to the broken walls and signalled other substances to come. These substances form strands called fibrin, which form a web over the red blood cells to create a clot. The scab is the clot on the skin.

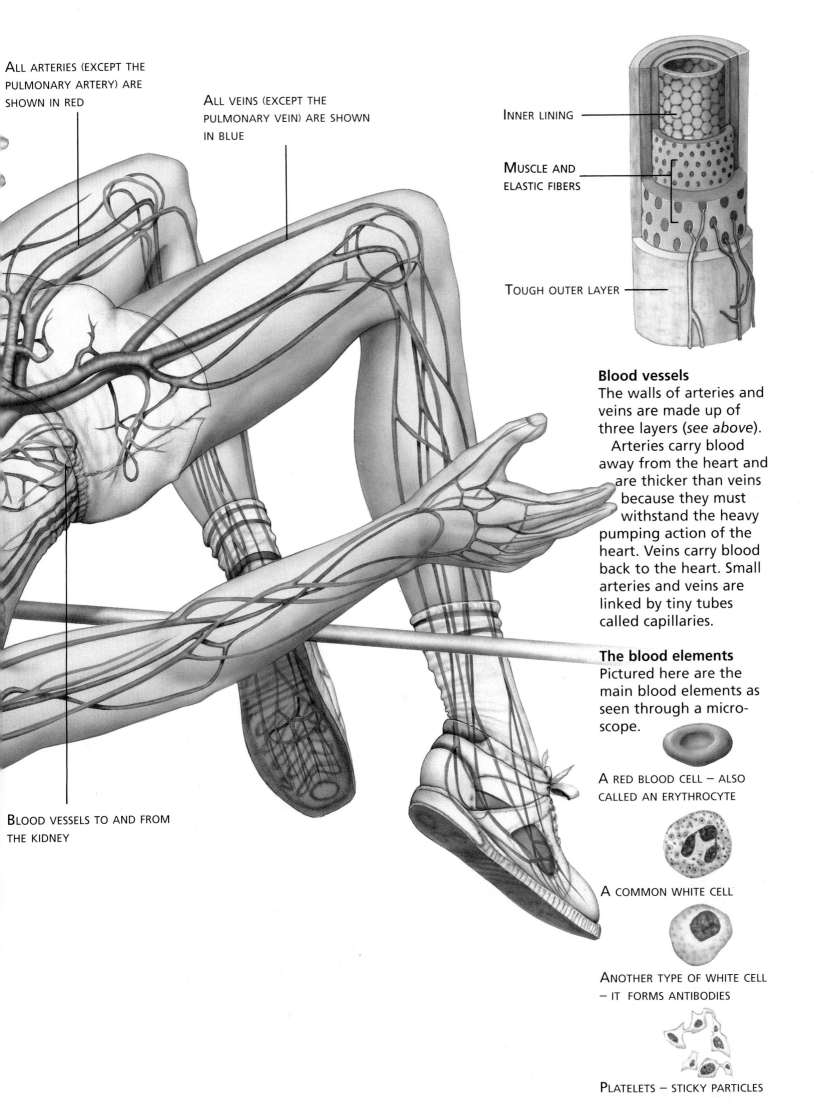

ALL ARTERIES (EXCEPT THE
PULMONARY ARTERY) ARE
SHOWN IN RED

ALL VEINS (EXCEPT THE
PULMONARY VEIN) ARE SHOWN
IN BLUE

INNER LINING

MUSCLE AND
ELASTIC FIBERS

TOUGH OUTER LAYER

Blood vessels
The walls of arteries and
veins are made up of
three layers (*see above*).
Arteries carry blood
away from the heart and
are thicker than veins
because they must
withstand the heavy
pumping action of the
heart. Veins carry blood
back to the heart. Small
arteries and veins are
linked by tiny tubes
called capillaries.

The blood elements
Pictured here are the
main blood elements as
seen through a micro-
scope.

A RED BLOOD CELL – ALSO
CALLED AN ERYTHROCYTE

A COMMON WHITE CELL

ANOTHER TYPE OF WHITE CELL
– IT FORMS ANTIBODIES

PLATELETS – STICKY PARTICLES

BLOOD VESSELS TO AND FROM
THE KIDNEY

11

The Heart

OUR HEART is the pump at the center of our blood system. Heart muscle is very strong as it has to pump blood through networks of small blood vessels around the body. Heart muscle contracts automatically; the number of times it contracts, or beats, in a minute is known as the heart rate. An adult normally has a heart rate of about 70 beats a minute. At birth our heart rate is much faster than this – sometimes twice as fast. Even as children our heart rate is usually about 100 beats per minute. Everyone's normal heart rate will increase if they exercise, because more oxygen, carried by the blood, is needed by hard-working muscles.

You can measure your heart rate by feeling your pulse. Your wrist is the best place to find it. If you put two fingers across the underside of your wrist, where the artery lies close to the surface of your skin, you can count the number of beats felt in one minute.

THE AORTA IS THE BIGGEST ARTERY IN THE BODY

SUPERIOR VENA CAVA

PULMONARY ARTERIES TAKE BLOOD TO THE LUNGS TO BE RE-OXYGENATED

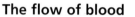

The flow of blood

The diagrams below show the direction that blood flows through the heart. The pulmonary veins carry blood rich in oxygen from the lungs to the left atrium (1). The blood then flows through the left ventricle (2) into the aorta (3). After this it is pumped around the body. At the same time that blood is leaving the heart, more blood is arriving at the right atrium through the large vein called the vena cava (1). This blood contains little oxygen because it has already been used by the body. Blood flows to the right ventricle (2) and then into the pulmonary artery to pick up more oxygen in the lungs (3). This cycle is repeated (4).

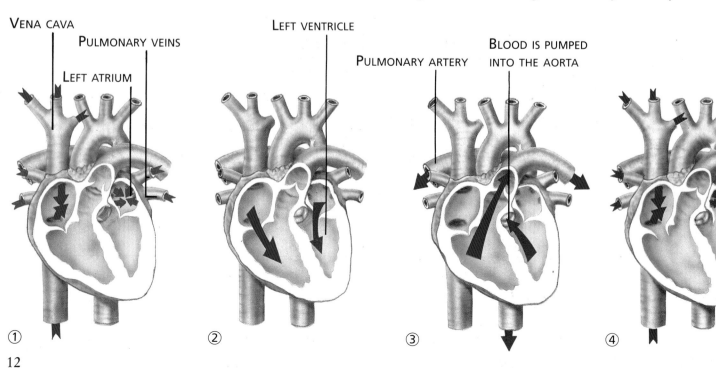

VENA CAVA
PULMONARY VEINS
LEFT ATRIUM
LEFT VENTRICLE
PULMONARY ARTERY
BLOOD IS PUMPED INTO THE AORTA

① ② ③ ④

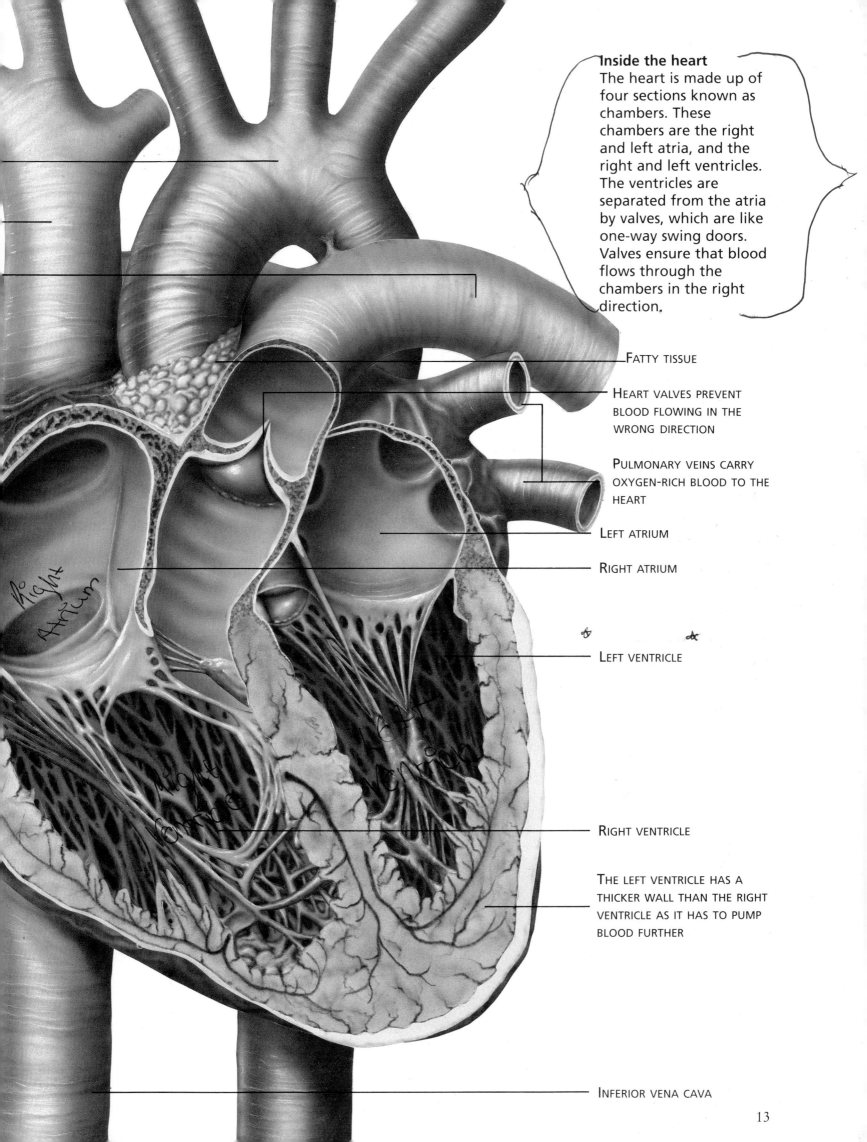

FATTY TISSUE

HEART VALVES PREVENT BLOOD FLOWING IN THE WRONG DIRECTION

PULMONARY VEINS CARRY OXYGEN-RICH BLOOD TO THE HEART

LEFT ATRIUM

RIGHT ATRIUM

LEFT VENTRICLE

RIGHT VENTRICLE

THE LEFT VENTRICLE HAS A THICKER WALL THAN THE RIGHT VENTRICLE AS IT HAS TO PUMP BLOOD FURTHER

INFERIOR VENA CAVA

13

Breathing

EVERY time you breathe, you draw in air containing a gas called oxygen, which makes your body work. Most adults breathe 18 times a minute – children breathe faster. When you breathe in, hairs in your nose, and mucus in your nose and throat, stop harmful particles of dust or bacteria from entering your lungs. The air then travels down the trachea (windpipe) and into your lungs through the left and right bronchi. Your ribs move outward and your diaphragm muscle moves down, allowing your lungs to expand and fill with air. The opposite happens when you breathe out.

BRONCHIOLE

ALVEOLI
(AIR SACS)

INSIDE AN ALVEOLUS

CAPILLARIES

ALVEOLUS WALL

CARBON
DIOXIDE

OXYGEN

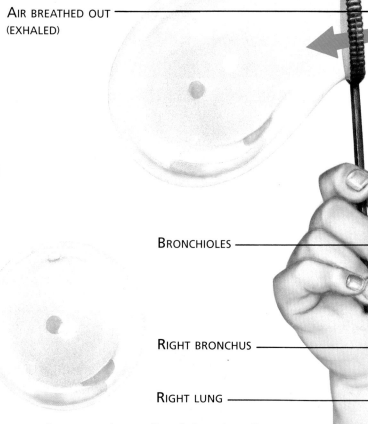

AIR BREATHED OUT
(EXHALED)

BRONCHIOLES

RIGHT BRONCHUS

RIGHT LUNG

How oxygen passes into the blood stream

The inside of a lung looks something like a large sponge. The left and right bronchi branch into thousands of small bronchioles, which end in tiny air sacs, called alveoli. These alveoli are surrounded by very fine blood vessels called capillaries. When we breathe in, the oxygen in the air passes through the walls of the alveoli, which are thinner than tissue paper, into the capillaries. The oxygen in the blood is then transported to cells around the body. Carbon dioxide, a waste gas, is transported in the opposite direction, from the cells to the walls of the alveoli. We get rid of carbon dioxide in our bodies when we breathe out.

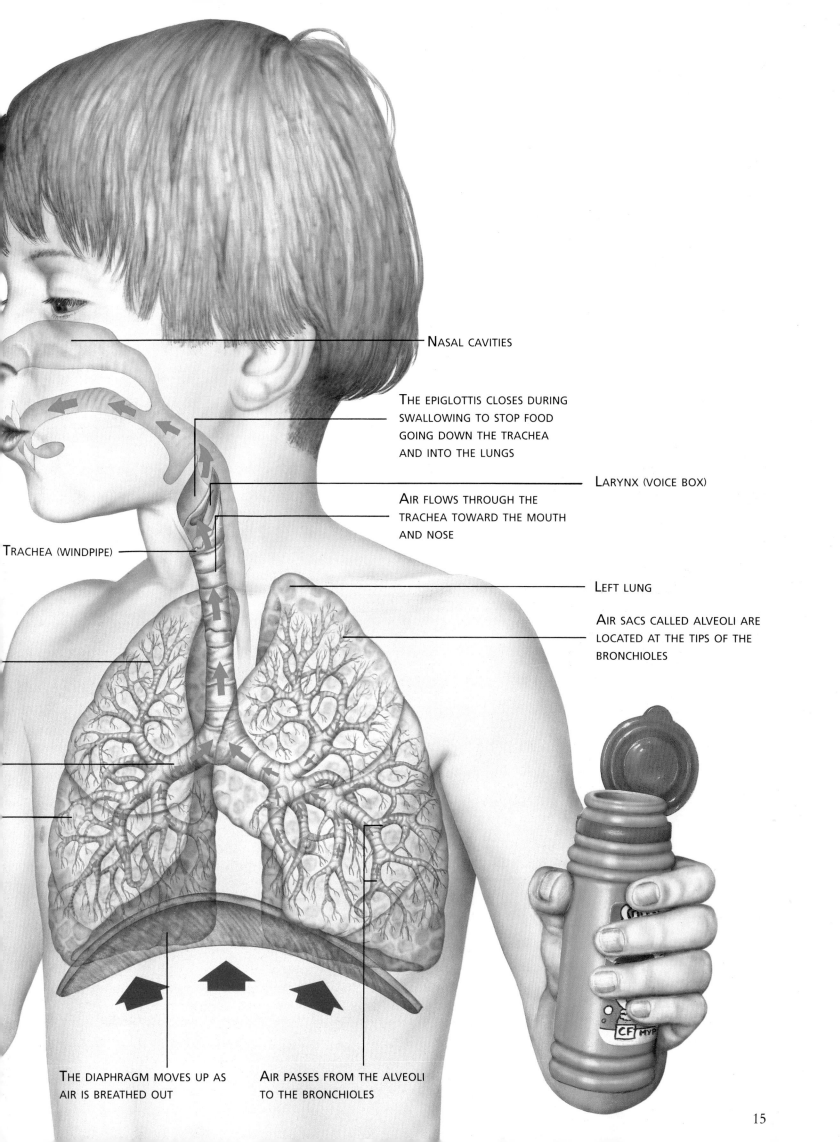

Nasal cavities

The epiglottis closes during
swallowing to stop food
going down the trachea
and into the lungs

Larynx (voice box)

Air flows through the
trachea toward the mouth
and nose

Trachea (windpipe)

Left lung

Air sacs called alveoli are
located at the tips of the
bronchioles

The diaphragm moves up as
air is breathed out

Air passes from the alveoli
to the bronchioles

15

The Skeleton

THE HUMAN skeleton is made up of more than 200 bones. It gives our muscles a firm place to anchor themselves and also protects our body's more fragile organs. For example, the brain is protected by the skull and the lungs are protected by the ribs. The bones of our skeleton vary in shape and size to fit their function. The spine has 33 separate bones. It is shaped to protect the spinal cord, which travels through it, while also giving the spinal muscles a place for attachment.

The male skeleton is different to the female skeleton. For example, the female pelvis is specially designed to allow a baby's safe journey down the birth canal.

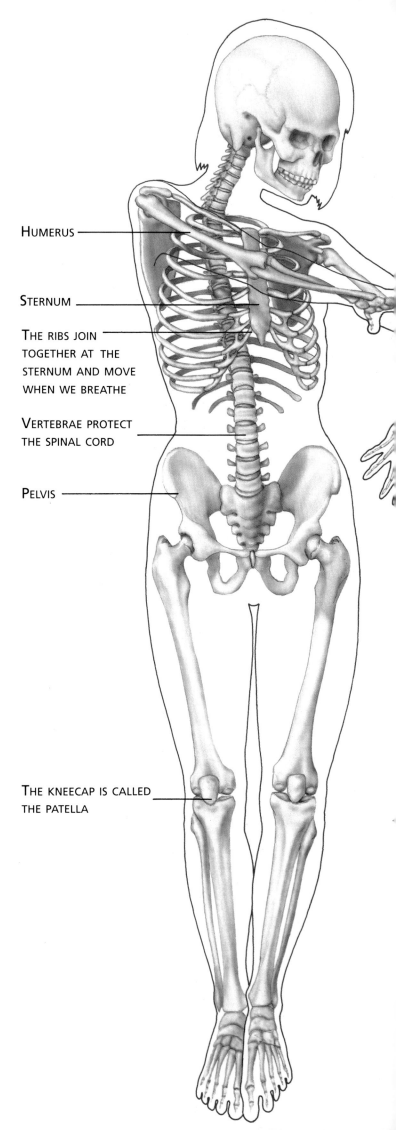

HUMERUS

STERNUM

THE RIBS JOIN TOGETHER AT THE STERNUM AND MOVE WHEN WE BREATHE

VERTEBRAE PROTECT THE SPINAL CORD

PELVIS

THE KNEECAP IS CALLED THE PATELLA

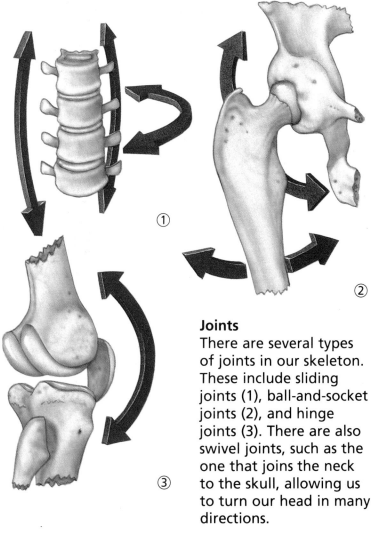

① ② ③

Joints
There are several types of joints in our skeleton. These include sliding joints (1), ball-and-socket joints (2), and hinge joints (3). There are also swivel joints, such as the one that joins the neck to the skull, allowing us to turn our head in many directions.

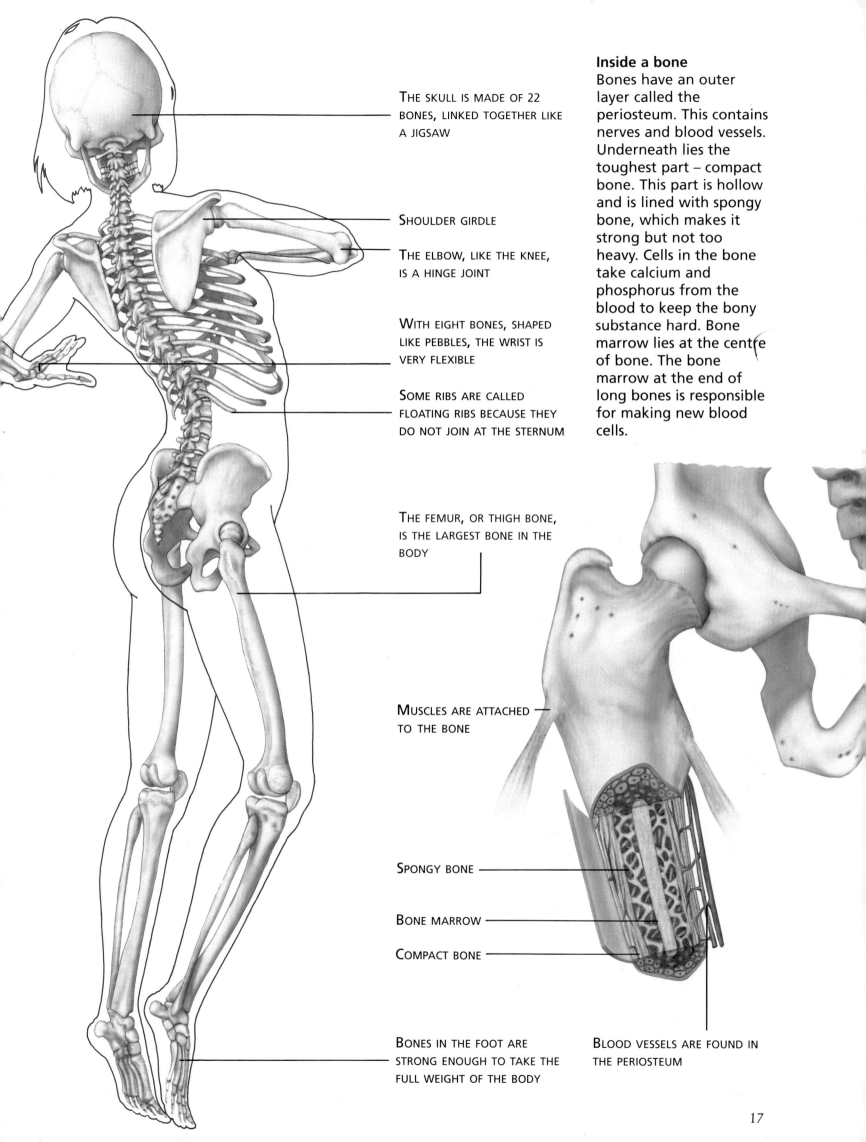

THE SKULL IS MADE OF 22 BONES, LINKED TOGETHER LIKE A JIGSAW

SHOULDER GIRDLE

THE ELBOW, LIKE THE KNEE, IS A HINGE JOINT

WITH EIGHT BONES, SHAPED LIKE PEBBLES, THE WRIST IS VERY FLEXIBLE

SOME RIBS ARE CALLED FLOATING RIBS BECAUSE THEY DO NOT JOIN AT THE STERNUM

THE FEMUR, OR THIGH BONE, IS THE LARGEST BONE IN THE BODY

MUSCLES ARE ATTACHED TO THE BONE

SPONGY BONE

BONE MARROW

COMPACT BONE

BONES IN THE FOOT ARE STRONG ENOUGH TO TAKE THE FULL WEIGHT OF THE BODY

BLOOD VESSELS ARE FOUND IN THE PERIOSTEUM

Inside a bone
Bones have an outer layer called the periosteum. This contains nerves and blood vessels. Underneath lies the toughest part – compact bone. This part is hollow and is lined with spongy bone, which makes it strong but not too heavy. Cells in the bone take calcium and phosphorus from the blood to keep the bony substance hard. Bone marrow lies at the centre of bone. The bone marrow at the end of long bones is responsible for making new blood cells.

17

Muscles

WE HAVE lots of muscles of different shapes and sizes, ranging from the large gluteus maximus on which we sit, to the tiny muscles that control the movements of our eyes. Many of our movements – when riding a bicycle, for example – involve a number of muscles that have to work together, and these are controlled by the brain. Every muscle in our body is made up of muscle fibers. Messages from the brain can make muscle fibers contract, making them shorter. As they shorten they become more powerful and are able to pull the bones to which they are attached. This causes movement.

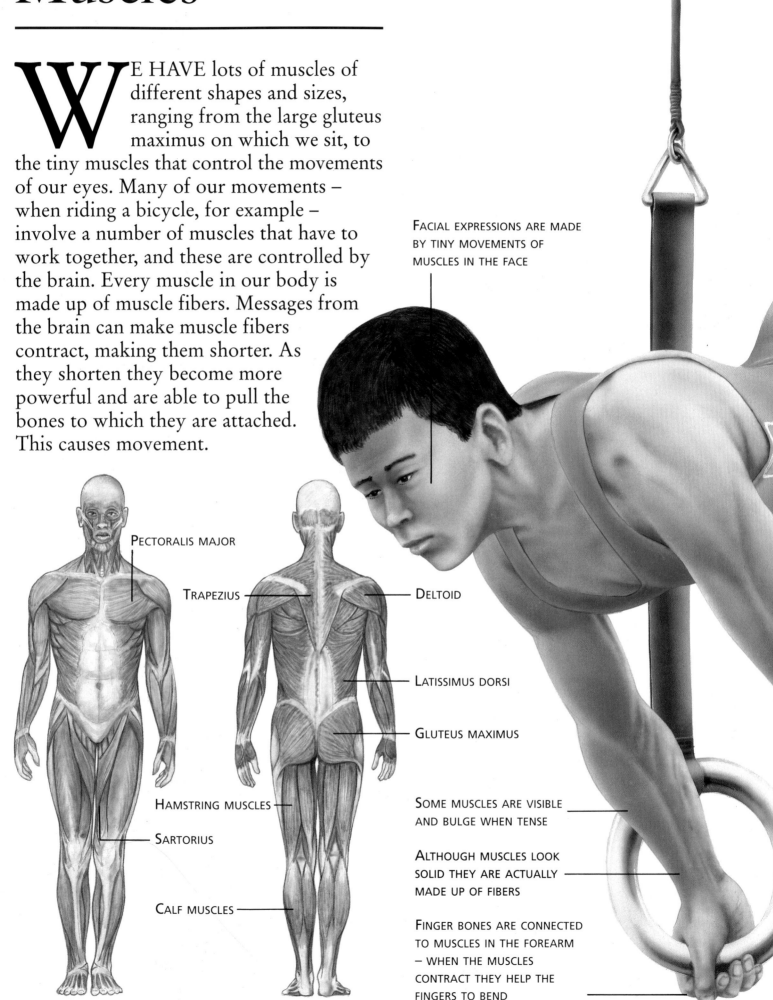

FACIAL EXPRESSIONS ARE MADE BY TINY MOVEMENTS OF MUSCLES IN THE FACE

PECTORALIS MAJOR

TRAPEZIUS

DELTOID

LATISSIMUS DORSI

GLUTEUS MAXIMUS

HAMSTRING MUSCLES

SARTORIUS

CALF MUSCLES

SOME MUSCLES ARE VISIBLE AND BULGE WHEN TENSE

ALTHOUGH MUSCLES LOOK SOLID THEY ARE ACTUALLY MADE UP OF FIBERS

FINGER BONES ARE CONNECTED TO MUSCLES IN THE FOREARM – WHEN THE MUSCLES CONTRACT THEY HELP THE FINGERS TO BEND

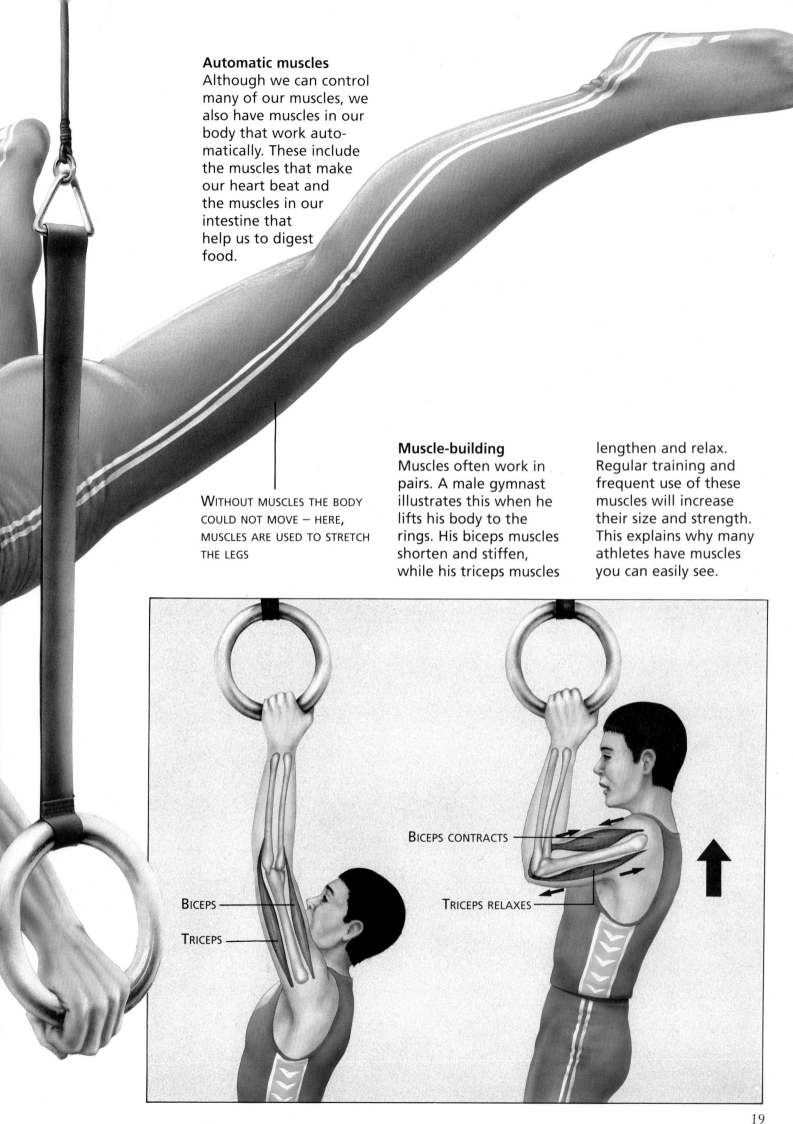

Automatic muscles
Although we can control many of our muscles, we also have muscles in our body that work automatically. These include the muscles that make our heart beat and the muscles in our intestine that help us to digest food.

WITHOUT MUSCLES THE BODY COULD NOT MOVE – HERE, MUSCLES ARE USED TO STRETCH THE LEGS

Muscle-building
Muscles often work in pairs. A male gymnast illustrates this when he lifts his body to the rings. His biceps muscles shorten and stiffen, while his triceps muscles lengthen and relax. Regular training and frequent use of these muscles will increase their size and strength. This explains why many athletes have muscles you can easily see.

BICEPS

TRICEPS

BICEPS CONTRACTS

TRICEPS RELAXES

The Digestive System

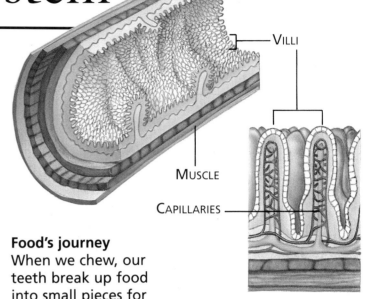

VILLI

MUSCLE

CAPILLARIES

WE NEED food in order to live; it is the fuel for our body's energy and growth. There are three main kinds of food: protein (found in meat, cheese, and nuts, for example), carbohydrates (found in bread and potatoes), and fat (found in oils and butter). Proteins are used for repairing the body and for growing; carbohydrates and fats are needed for providing energy.

Digestion is a process that begins when we put food in our mouths and ends when the food has been absorbed into the bloodstream. It takes up to eighteen hours for digestion to occur. This is not surprising because our food has to travel through more than 26 feet of coiled-up tubing called the small intestine. On its journey food gets broken down by acid and enzymes. An enzyme is a chemical that changes food into a substance we can easily absorb.

Food's journey
When we chew, our teeth break up food into small pieces for swallowing. Food then travels down a muscular tube called the esophagus, to the stomach, which is a bag containing acid that kills off any bacteria (1). Next, food enters the small intestine (2). There it is broken up into useful substances and waste substances by enzymes, which are produced by a gland called the pancreas.

Inside the small intestine finger-like bumps, known as villi, contain blood vessels that absorb the useful substances into the bloodstream. Waste substances remain and pass into the large intestine, where water is absorbed until the waste becomes solid (3). This waste is later expelled from the rectum.

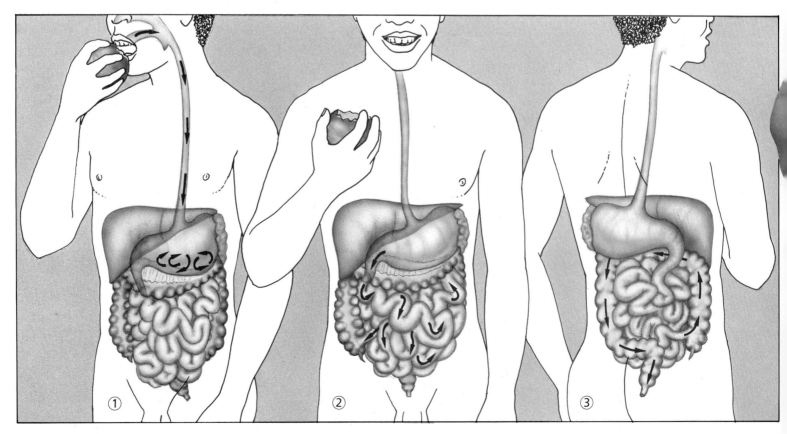

① ② ③

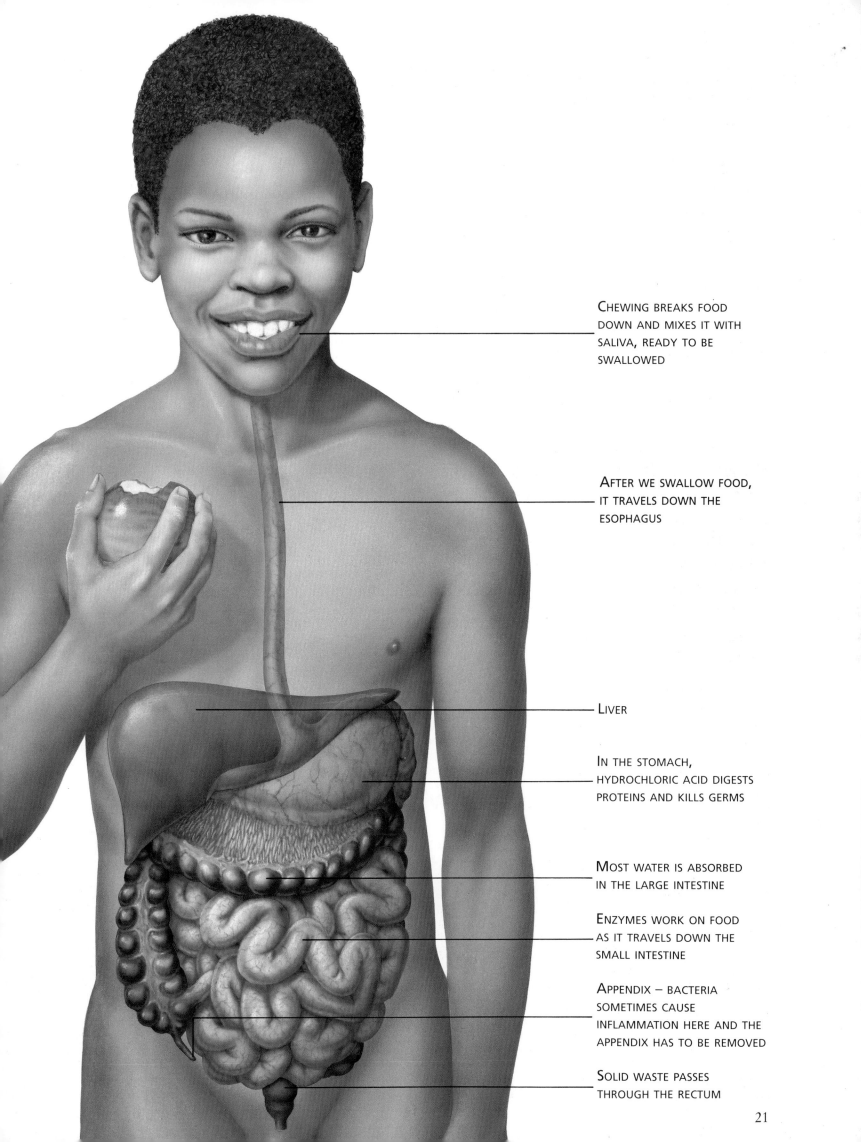

CHEWING BREAKS FOOD
DOWN AND MIXES IT WITH
SALIVA, READY TO BE
SWALLOWED

AFTER WE SWALLOW FOOD,
IT TRAVELS DOWN THE
ESOPHAGUS

LIVER

IN THE STOMACH,
HYDROCHLORIC ACID DIGESTS
PROTEINS AND KILLS GERMS

MOST WATER IS ABSORBED
IN THE LARGE INTESTINE

ENZYMES WORK ON FOOD
AS IT TRAVELS DOWN THE
SMALL INTESTINE

APPENDIX – BACTERIA
SOMETIMES CAUSE
INFLAMMATION HERE AND THE
APPENDIX HAS TO BE REMOVED

SOLID WASTE PASSES
THROUGH THE RECTUM

Teeth

TEETH are designed to break food into small, soft pieces for swallowing. The teeth at the front of the mouth, called incisors, are used for cutting. Behind these are the canine teeth, which are especially good for tearing tough food. The flatter teeth at the back are called premolars and molars; they are used for grinding and mashing.

Our first set of teeth, known as 'milk teeth', appear in infancy. The very first tooth usually appears at about seven months of age and is one of the lower incisors. The upper teeth appear two months later and the premolars appear around our first birthday. A second set of teeth grows, replacing our milk teeth, from about the age of six (*see below*). These teeth are complete when the 'wisdom teeth', which are molars at the back of the gums, come through at around the age of 20. In total an adult has 32 teeth.

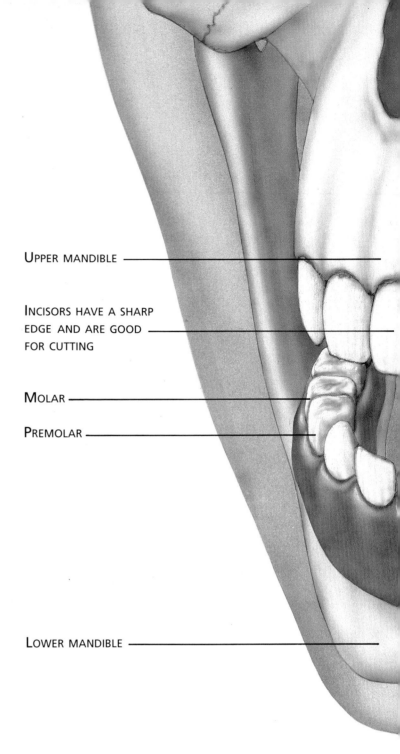

UPPER MANDIBLE

INCISORS HAVE A SHARP EDGE AND ARE GOOD FOR CUTTING

MOLAR

PREMOLAR

LOWER MANDIBLE

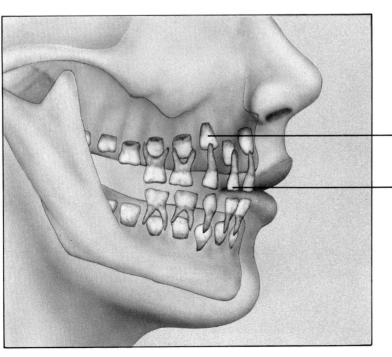

PERMANENT TEETH WAITING TO BREAK THROUGH

MILK TEETH ARE SLOWLY PUSHED OUT

Tooth decay
A tooth has two parts: the crown and the root. The crown is the visible part above the gum and the root is the part that lies hidden in the gum. The crown is covered in enamel – the hardest substance of the body – which helps to protect the fragile blood vessels and nerves that lie inside the tooth. Dentine, another hard layer, surrounds and protects

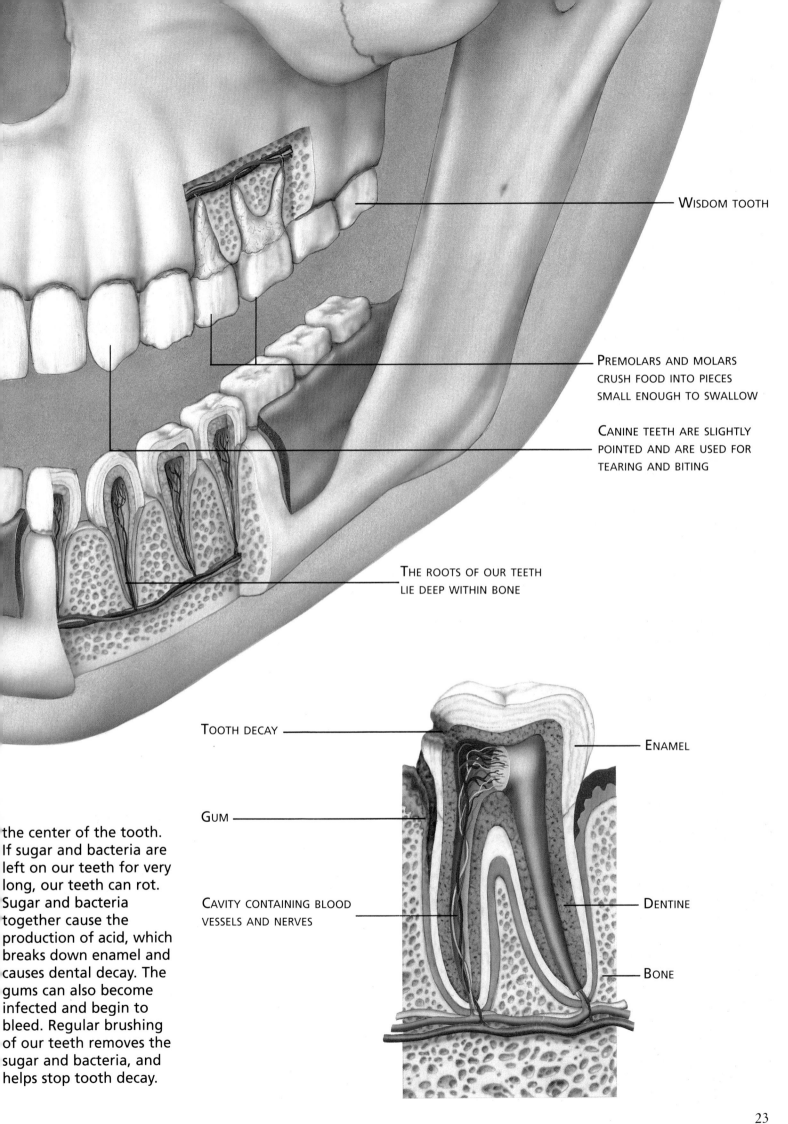

WISDOM TOOTH

PREMOLARS AND MOLARS
CRUSH FOOD INTO PIECES
SMALL ENOUGH TO SWALLOW

CANINE TEETH ARE SLIGHTLY
POINTED AND ARE USED FOR
TEARING AND BITING

THE ROOTS OF OUR TEETH
LIE DEEP WITHIN BONE

TOOTH DECAY

ENAMEL

GUM

the center of the tooth.
If sugar and bacteria are
left on our teeth for very
long, our teeth can rot.
Sugar and bacteria
together cause the
production of acid, which
breaks down enamel and
causes dental decay. The
gums can also become
infected and begin to
bleed. Regular brushing
of our teeth removes the
sugar and bacteria, and
helps stop tooth decay.

CAVITY CONTAINING BLOOD
VESSELS AND NERVES

DENTINE

BONE

23

The Liver and Kidneys

THE LIVER is the blood's cleaning and sorting center. A vein called the portal vein connects the intestines directly to the liver, bringing to the liver blood that is rich in dissolved food. The liver sorts through the blood, taking out harmful chemical waste and storing useful substances, such as sugars and vitamins.

When the kidneys receive blood containing waste substances, they filter and remove these substances together with any excess water. The kidneys pass this waste, or urine, to the bladder, and pass the filtered, clean blood back to the heart.

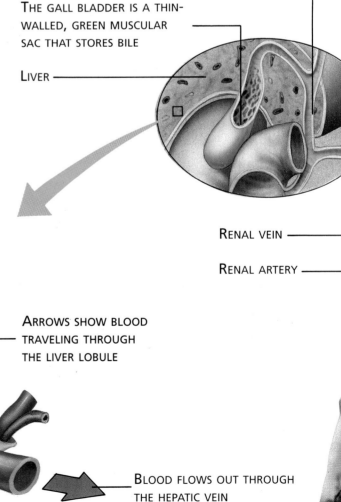

FLUID IS ESSENTIAL FOR THE BODY TO FUNCTION

THE COMMON BILE DUCT JOINS THE GALL-BLADDER TO THE INTESTINE

THE GALL BLADDER IS A THIN-WALLED, GREEN MUSCULAR SAC THAT STORES BILE

LIVER

RENAL VEIN

RENAL ARTERY

Liver lobule

Our liver is made up of small structures called lobules. Each lobule contains spaces through which blood flows. Some of the chemical waste in the blood is removed, turned into bile, and stored in the gall bladder. Bile removes waste and makes fats soluble for absorption.

BLOOD FLOWS IN THROUGH THE PORTAL VEIN

BILE NETWORK

ARROWS SHOW BLOOD TRAVELING THROUGH THE LIVER LOBULE

BLOOD FLOWS OUT THROUGH THE HEPATIC VEIN

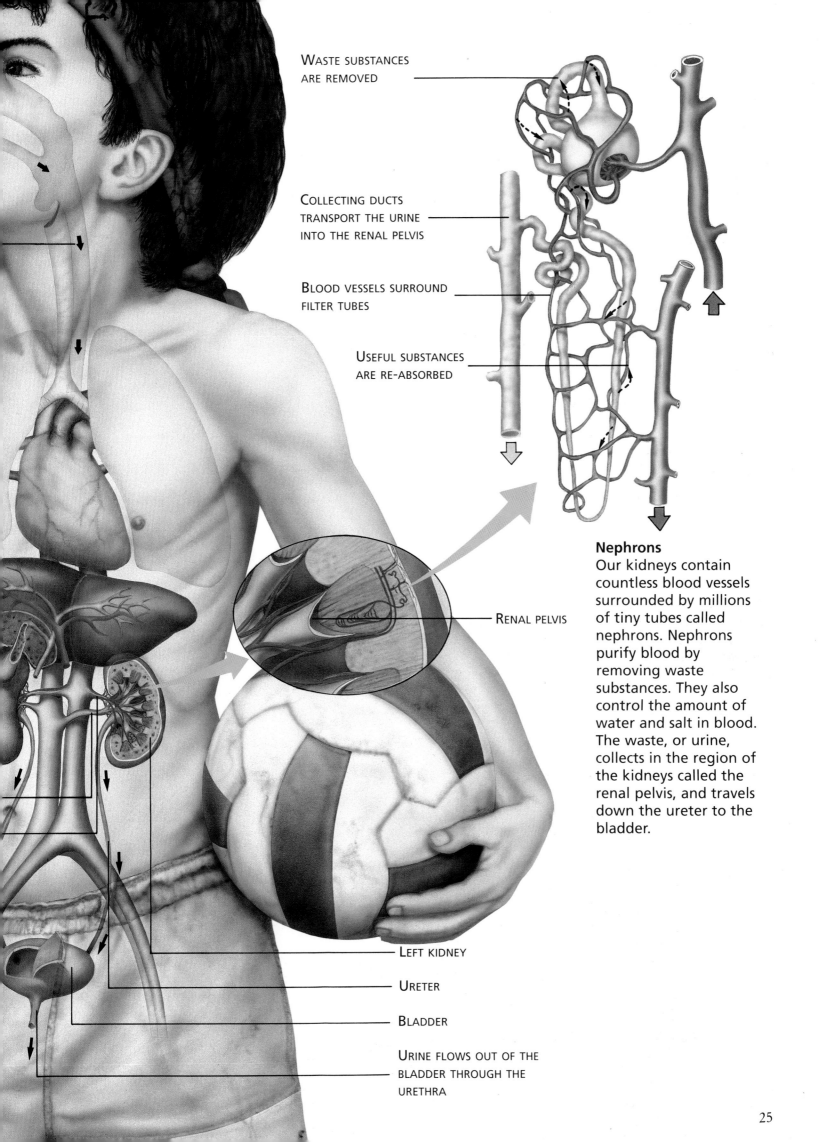

WASTE SUBSTANCES
ARE REMOVED

COLLECTING DUCTS
TRANSPORT THE URINE
INTO THE RENAL PELVIS

BLOOD VESSELS SURROUND
FILTER TUBES

USEFUL SUBSTANCES
ARE RE-ABSORBED

RENAL PELVIS

Nephrons
Our kidneys contain
countless blood vessels
surrounded by millions
of tiny tubes called
nephrons. Nephrons
purify blood by
removing waste
substances. They also
control the amount of
water and salt in blood.
The waste, or urine,
collects in the region of
the kidneys called the
renal pelvis, and travels
down the ureter to the
bladder.

LEFT KIDNEY

URETER

BLADDER

URINE FLOWS OUT OF THE
BLADDER THROUGH THE
URETHRA

The Skin

SKIN IS OUR protective coat – a complex covering of two layers. The top layer is the epidermis, which as well as being waterproof also protects us against germs. The cells in this layer are being shed all the time, with new cells growing in their place. The dermis layer beneath is much thicker, and is made up of elastic fibers. It contains blood vessels, sweat glands, and hair roots, called follicles. These all help to control our body temperature. In hot weather the blood vessels widen and allow more blood to flow near the cooler surface of the skin. Sweat glands produce salty droplets that evaporate on the body and cool it down. In cold weather muscles attached to hair follicles tighten, making our hairs stand on end. This traps a thin layer of warm air around the body. In addition, blood vessels narrow to keep the body's heat in and away from the skin's surface.

The sun
Our skin is delicate and very sensitive to the sun. Ultraviolet rays produced by the sun shine on our skin and can cause the skin to burn. This often results in painful blistering red skin. Sometimes the sun's rays can actually cause cells in our skin to change and skin cancer to develop.

Everybody needs to protect their skin from the sun either by staying in the shade or by using sun cream. Sun cream contains substances that help block out the harmful rays. Wearing a hat also helps to protect our face and neck, and wearing light clothing keeps the sun away from our skin.

EPIDERMIS – THIS IS THE GERMPROOF AND WATERPROOF LAYER

MELANIN – THE PIGMENT THAT GIVES SKIN A BROWN COLOR

SENSORY NERVE ENDINGS

THE DERMIS LAYER CONTAINS FIBERS THAT MAKE SKIN SUPPLE AND ELASTIC

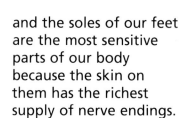

FATTY CELLS TO KEEP US WARM

NERVE FIBERS IN THE SKIN

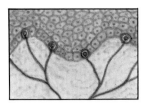

FOR PAIN

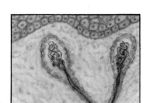

FOR TOUCH

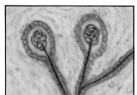

FOR COLD TEMPERATURE

FOR PRESSURE

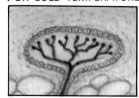

FOR HEAT

Sensitive skin
Nerve endings in the dermis enable us to feel heat, cold, pain, and pressure. They also help protect our bodies from damage. Our hands, lips, and the soles of our feet are the most sensitive parts of our body because the skin on them has the richest supply of nerve endings.

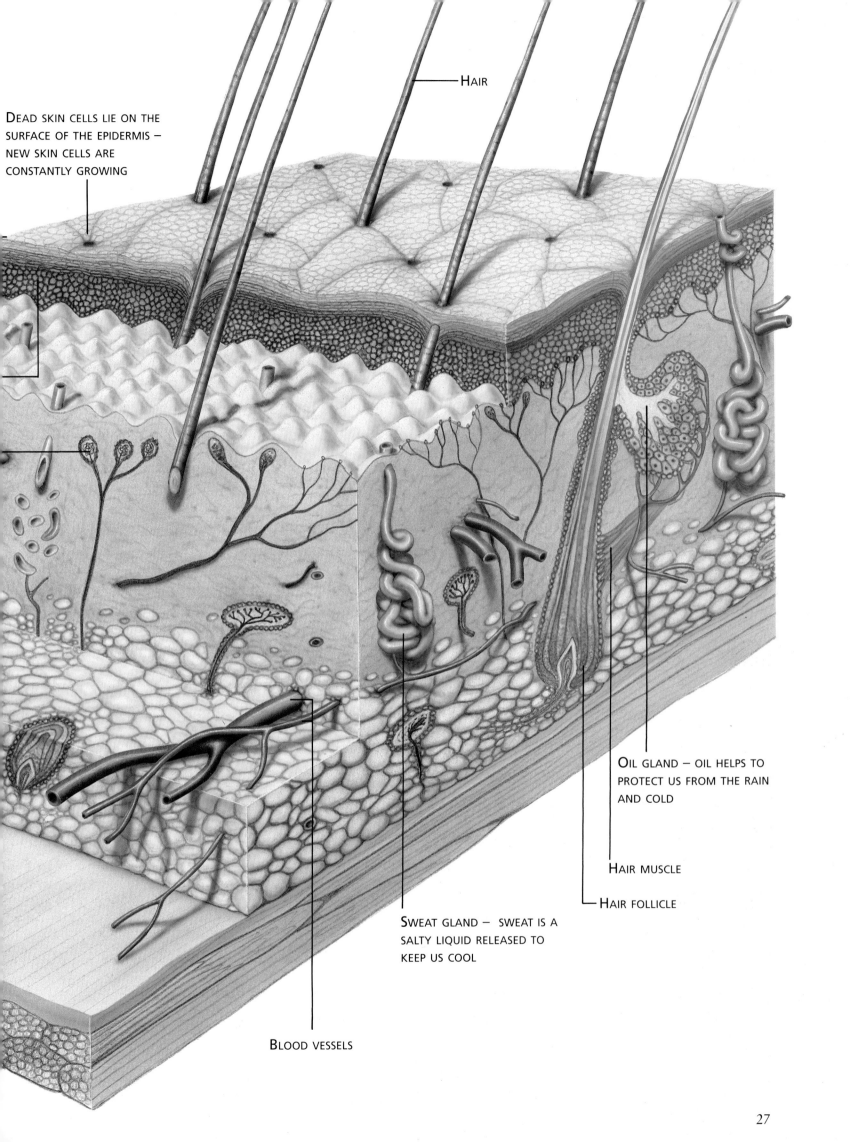

HAIR

DEAD SKIN CELLS LIE ON THE
SURFACE OF THE EPIDERMIS –
NEW SKIN CELLS ARE
CONSTANTLY GROWING

OIL GLAND – OIL HELPS TO
PROTECT US FROM THE RAIN
AND COLD

HAIR MUSCLE

HAIR FOLLICLE

SWEAT GLAND – SWEAT IS A
SALTY LIQUID RELEASED TO
KEEP US COOL

BLOOD VESSELS

The Nerves

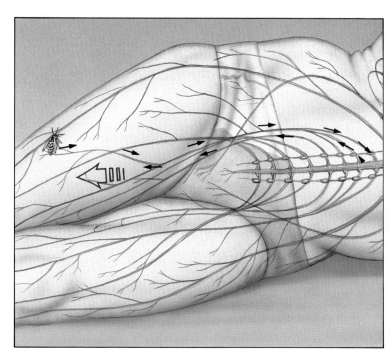

OUR NERVOUS system is a busy network of nerves. It includes the nerves in our brain and the nerves that stretch throughout our bodies. Our brain is connected to the rest of our body by the spinal cord, a thick cable that runs down the spinal column in our back.

Nerves are made up of thin strands called neurons. There are millions of these throughout the nervous system and each consists of a cell body, which has short branches called dendrites. The long arm of the neuron is called the axon. Some axons are enclosed in a fatty layer called myelin, which helps to speed up the conduction, or passing, of nerve messages along the axon. Nerve cells in our spinal cord cannot be replaced, so spinal injury can be serious.

The reflex action
The sensory impulse travels up the leg and into the spinal cord. It is then transmitted to neurons in the gray matter of the cord, which link up with motor neurons. The impulse travels back down the leg in the motor nerve, and the leg muscle tightens, making the leg jerk. The reflex action does not involve the brain.

A wasp sting
When a wasp stings (*see left*), nerve endings in the area are excited and a nerve message, called an impulse, is sent along a nerve. Nerves carrying sensations, such as pain, are known as sensory nerves.

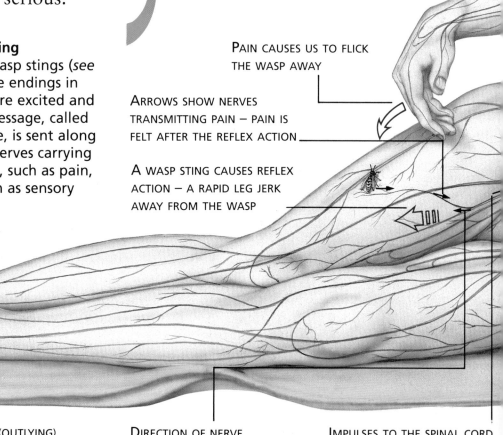

PAIN CAUSES US TO FLICK THE WASP AWAY

ARROWS SHOW NERVES TRANSMITTING PAIN – PAIN IS FELT AFTER THE REFLEX ACTION

A WASP STING CAUSES REFLEX ACTION – A RAPID LEG JERK AWAY FROM THE WASP

PERIPHERAL (OUTLYING) NERVES

DIRECTION OF NERVE MESSAGES, OR IMPULSES

IMPULSES TO THE SPINAL CORD AND BRAIN TRAVEL ALONG SENSORY NERVES

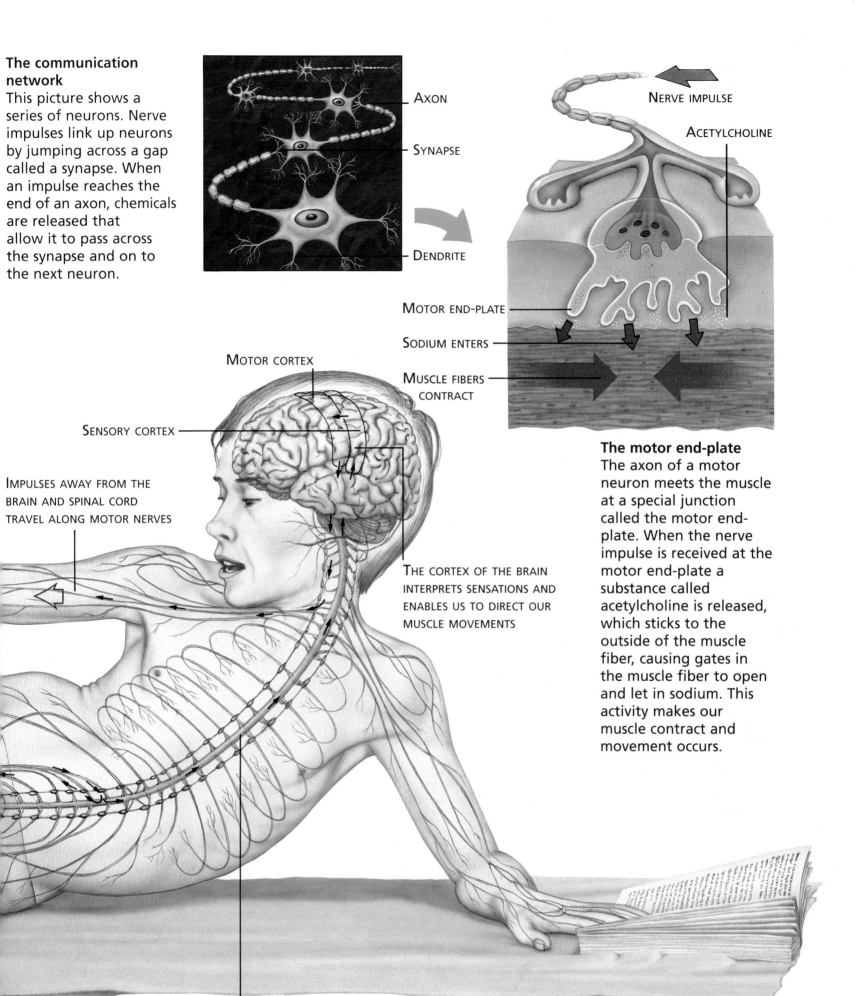

The communication network
This picture shows a series of neurons. Nerve impulses link up neurons by jumping across a gap called a synapse. When an impulse reaches the end of an axon, chemicals are released that allow it to pass across the synapse and on to the next neuron.

AXON

SYNAPSE

DENDRITE

NERVE IMPULSE

ACETYLCHOLINE

MOTOR END-PLATE

SODIUM ENTERS

MUSCLE FIBERS CONTRACT

MOTOR CORTEX

SENSORY CORTEX

IMPULSES AWAY FROM THE BRAIN AND SPINAL CORD TRAVEL ALONG MOTOR NERVES

THE CORTEX OF THE BRAIN INTERPRETS SENSATIONS AND ENABLES US TO DIRECT OUR MUSCLE MOVEMENTS

SPINAL CORD

The motor end-plate
The axon of a motor neuron meets the muscle at a special junction called the motor end-plate. When the nerve impulse is received at the motor end-plate a substance called acetylcholine is released, which sticks to the outside of the muscle fiber, causing gates in the muscle fiber to open and let in sodium. This activity makes our muscle contract and movement occurs.

The Brain

THE BRAIN looks like a mass of gray jelly and is very soft. It is protected in the hard, bony case known as the skull. The human brain is quite large but is wrinkled, which makes it compact.

The brain is the body's control center. It is involved with what we do and what we think, as well as what we feel and remember. We also use our brain to learn. The left-hand side of our brain controls the right side of the body, and the right-hand side of our brain controls the left side of the body. Most people are right handed, because the left side of the brain is generally used more than the right side. It has been found that each side of our brain is responsible for different skills. The right side holds our artistic talent and imagination, and the left side is more responsible for practical abilities and logical thinking.

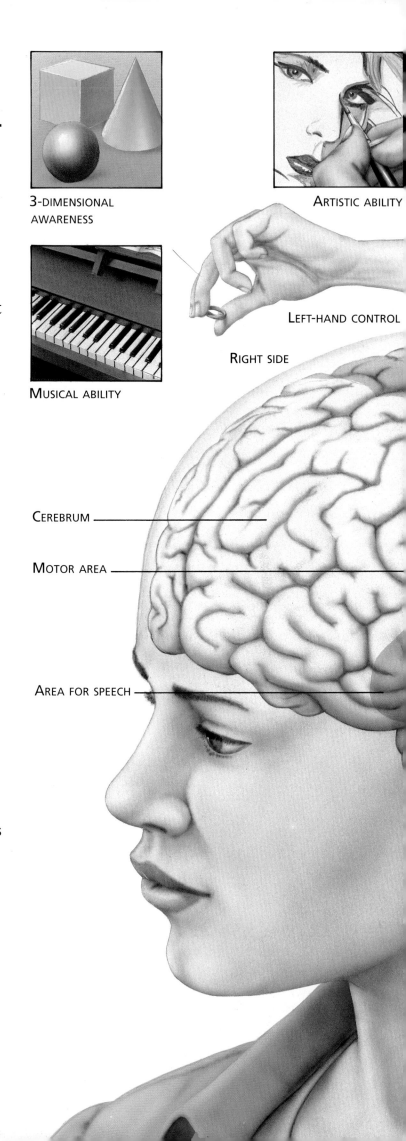

3-DIMENSIONAL AWARENESS

ARTISTIC ABILITY

LEFT-HAND CONTROL

RIGHT SIDE

MUSICAL ABILITY

CEREBRUM

MOTOR AREA

AREA FOR SPEECH

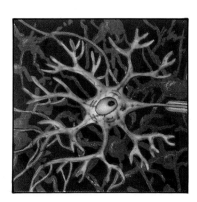

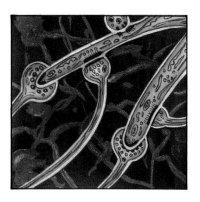

Brain cells
The cells that make up the brain are called neurons (*top left*). Branches from the cells, called dendrites, receive impulses from the nerves while axons transmit them (*bottom left*). Our brain interprets the impulses and can tell where they are coming from and to what they are referring. The brain cells can also store information. A piece of stored information is called a memory. One part of our brain stores long-term memories, another part more recent memories.

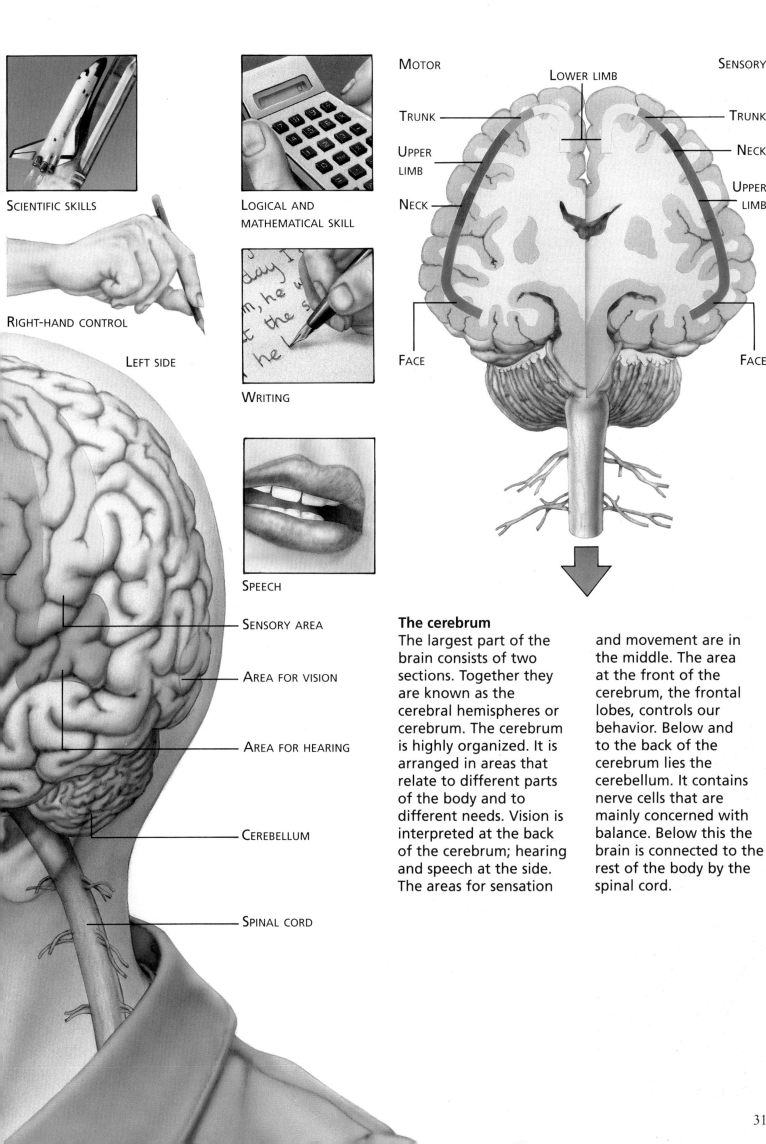

SCIENTIFIC SKILLS

LOGICAL AND MATHEMATICAL SKILL

RIGHT-HAND CONTROL

LEFT SIDE

WRITING

SPEECH

SENSORY AREA

AREA FOR VISION

AREA FOR HEARING

CEREBELLUM

SPINAL CORD

MOTOR

LOWER LIMB

TRUNK

UPPER LIMB

NECK

FACE

SENSORY

TRUNK

NECK

UPPER LIMB

FACE

The cerebrum

The largest part of the brain consists of two sections. Together they are known as the cerebral hemispheres or cerebrum. The cerebrum is highly organized. It is arranged in areas that relate to different parts of the body and to different needs. Vision is interpreted at the back of the cerebrum; hearing and speech at the side. The areas for sensation and movement are in the middle. The area at the front of the cerebrum, the frontal lobes, controls our behavior. Below and to the back of the cerebrum lies the cerebellum. It contains nerve cells that are mainly concerned with balance. Below this the brain is connected to the rest of the body by the spinal cord.

Seeing

OUR EYES work like cameras. Each eye has a pupil, which, similar to a camera's aperture, is a hole that allows light to enter the eye. When it is dark our pupils enlarge to let in as much light as possible. The size of each pupil is controlled by the iris, which surrounds it. When light passes through the pupil it meets the lens. The lens causes the light to bend so that it shines on an area at the back of the eye called the retina. The retina is something like the color film in a camera in that an image can be formed on it. This image is upside down and is transmitted by the optic nerve to the brain, which enables us to interpret it right-side up.

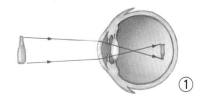

①

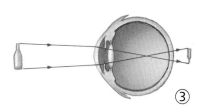

②

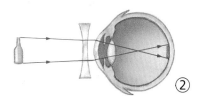

③

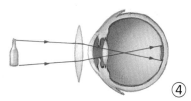

④

Focusing with glasses
A camera can be focused by moving the lens in and out, but the human eye focuses by making its lens thinner and longer or shorter and thicker. Some people's lenses will not focus properly, but they can be helped with glasses or contact lenses. These provide another lens through which the light can bend, allowing it to focus accurately on the retina. Short-sighted people cannot see distant images clearly because they focus them in front of the retina (1). Such people need concave lenses (2). Long-sighted people cannot see close images clearly because they focus them behind the retina (3). These people need convex lenses (4).

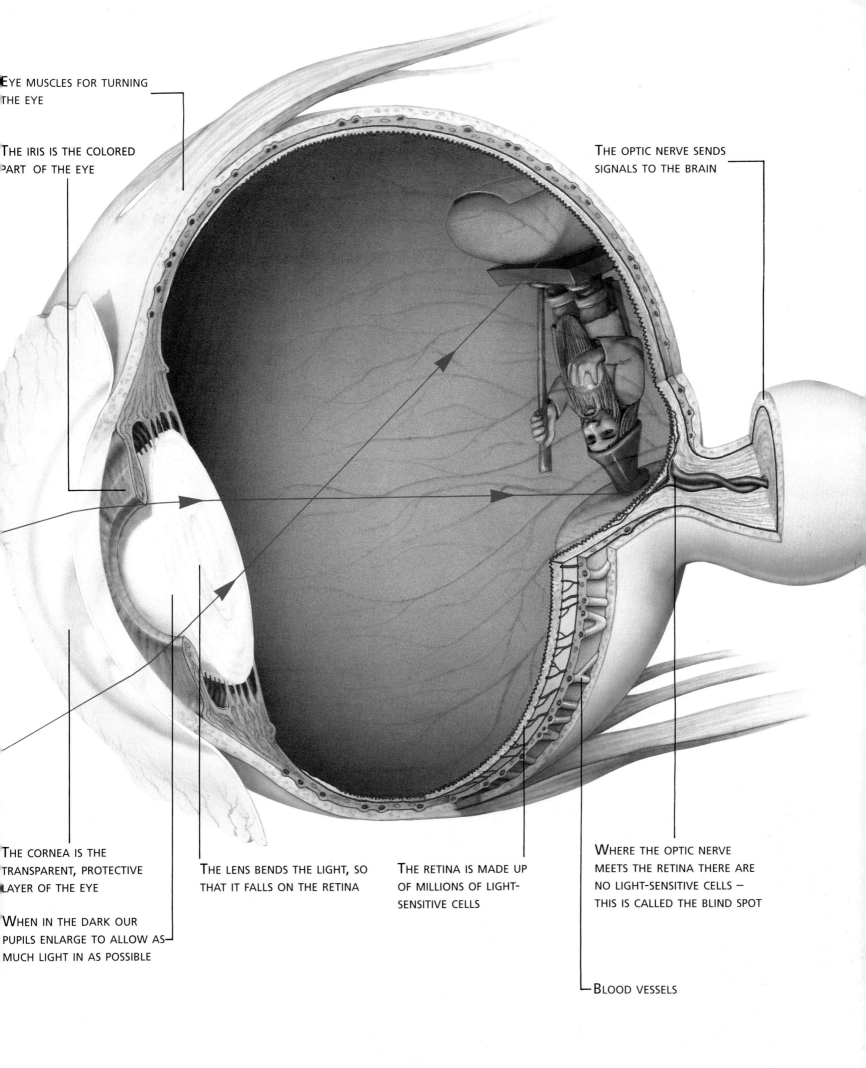

EYE MUSCLES FOR TURNING THE EYE

THE IRIS IS THE COLORED PART OF THE EYE

THE OPTIC NERVE SENDS SIGNALS TO THE BRAIN

THE CORNEA IS THE TRANSPARENT, PROTECTIVE LAYER OF THE EYE

WHEN IN THE DARK OUR PUPILS ENLARGE TO ALLOW AS MUCH LIGHT IN AS POSSIBLE

THE LENS BENDS THE LIGHT, SO THAT IT FALLS ON THE RETINA

THE RETINA IS MADE UP OF MILLIONS OF LIGHT-SENSITIVE CELLS

WHERE THE OPTIC NERVE MEETS THE RETINA THERE ARE NO LIGHT-SENSITIVE CELLS – THIS IS CALLED THE BLIND SPOT

BLOOD VESSELS

Taste and Smell

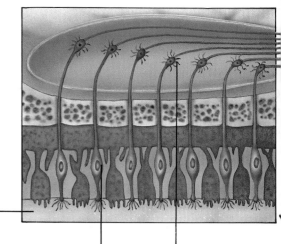

MUCUS LINING

NERVE FIBERS TO THE BRAIN

ODOR-SENSITIVE CELLS

WE ARE most familiar with the senses of taste and smell for the pleasure they can bring. However, they probably were developed to protect us from eating food that could be poisonous. Our sense of smell is much stronger than our sense of taste. When we taste food we rely on the smell and texture as well as the taste. This explains why we cannot taste food very well when we have a cold.

When eating a pear, for example, scent from the fruit rises up the nose and dissolves in a mucus lining that covers the scent-sensitive cells at the top of the nose. Nerve signals are sent from the cells to the olfactory lobe in the brain, where the smell is recognized and enjoyed. The pear's sweetness is also sensed by taste buds on the tongue, and is similarly transmitted by nerve signals to the brain.

Odor-sensitive cells
At the top of our nose lie special odor-sensitive cells that become stimulated when vapors are released from food, drinks, and the environment. These special cells are called olfactory cells and they contain hairs on which mucus lies. Vapors dissolve in the mucus, causing nerve impulses to be sent to the brain.

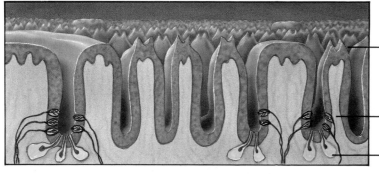

PAPILLAE COVER THE UPPER SURFACE OF THE TONGUE

TASTE BUDS

GLANDS SECRETE MUCUS

SCENT FROM THE PEAR IS BREATHED IN

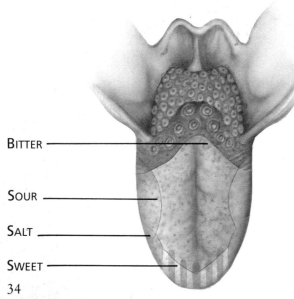

BITTER

SOUR

SALT

SWEET

Four kinds of taste
Our tongue contains about 10,000 taste buds, which pick up and respond to salt, sweet, sour, or bitter tastes. The taste buds are stimulated when chemicals from food are dissolved in the mouth's fluid – our saliva. Combined together, the four basic tastes give us a range of subtle flavors.

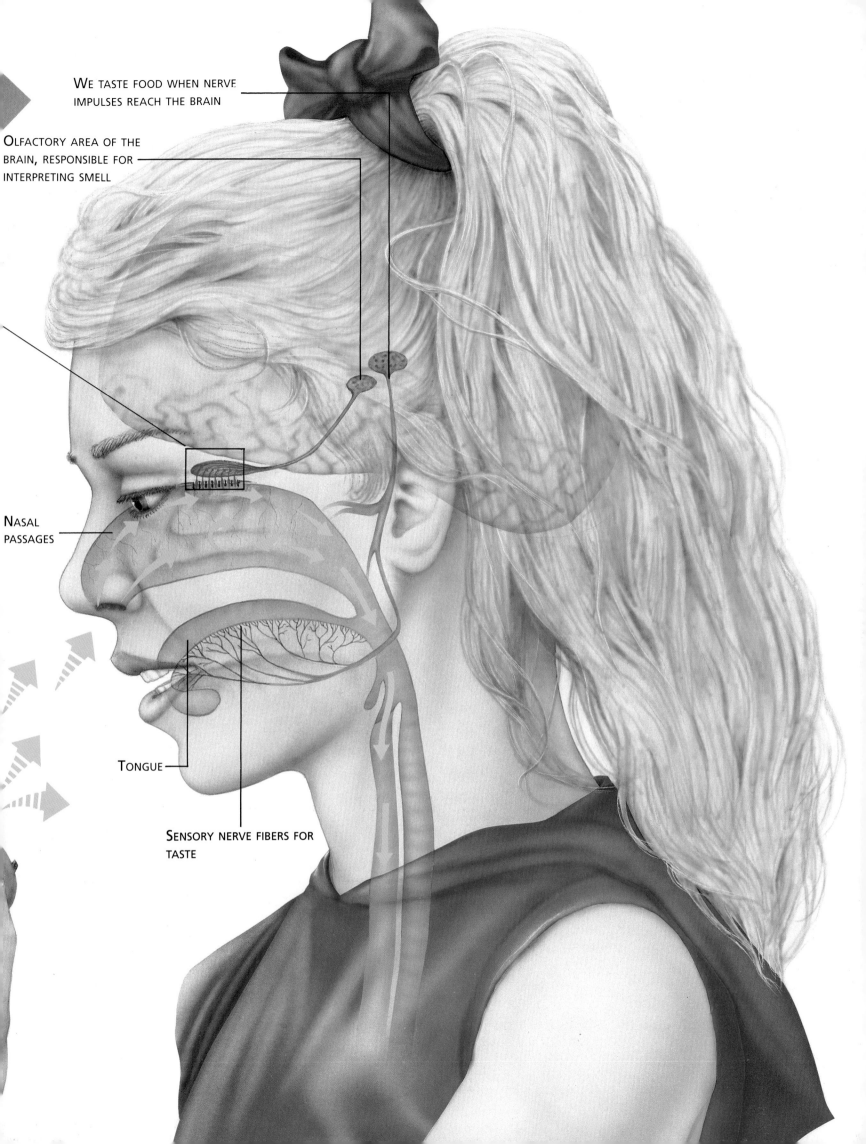

WE TASTE FOOD WHEN NERVE IMPULSES REACH THE BRAIN

OLFACTORY AREA OF THE BRAIN, RESPONSIBLE FOR INTERPRETING SMELL

NASAL PASSAGES

TONGUE

SENSORY NERVE FIBERS FOR TASTE

Hearing

THE PART of the ear we see is shaped to collect sound and allow it to travel along the ear canal to the eardrum. Sound causes the eardrum to vibrate. Behind the eardrum are three small bones called the hammer, anvil and stirrup, which get their names from their shapes. Vibrations from the eardrum cause the small bones to vibrate too, and these vibrations pass through an oval window to the cochlea. The cochlea is a coiled tube filled with liquid. Low-pitched sounds make the first part of the tube vibrate, while high-pitched sounds vibrate a part further up. These vibrations are picked up by nerve fibers connected to the brain. The brain can tell where the vibrations are occurring and so can tell one sound from another.

Balance and sound
Ears help us to balance. There are three semi-circular canals in the ear. They contain fluid that moves when we change our position. The moving fluid sends signals to the brain that helps our body to adjust and keep its sense of balance.

Our ears can endure very loud sounds, but if they are too loud, sounds can damage the cochlea. Soft sounds become more difficult to hear as we get older. We can hear low- and high-pitched sounds, although many animals, such as bats, can hear even higher-pitched sounds than we can.

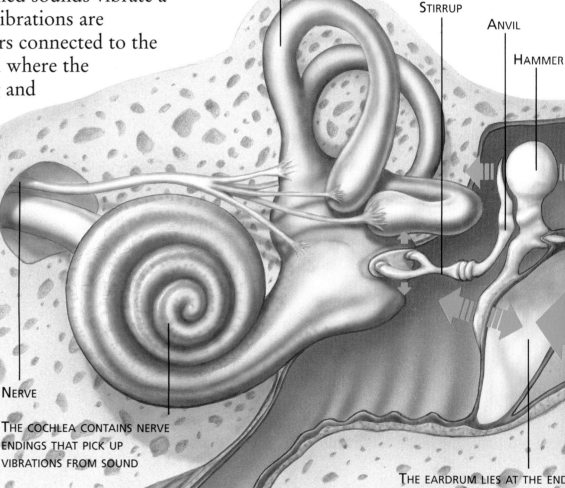

SEMICIRCULAR CANALS CONTAIN FLUID AND NERVE CELLS THAT ARE SENSITIVE TO MOVEMENT AND HELP US TO KEEP OUR BALANCE

STIRRUP

ANVIL

HAMMER

SOUND SIGNALS TRAVEL TO THE BRAIN

NERVE

THE COCHLEA CONTAINS NERVE ENDINGS THAT PICK UP VIBRATIONS FROM SOUND

THE EARDRUM LIES AT THE END OF THE EAR CANAL

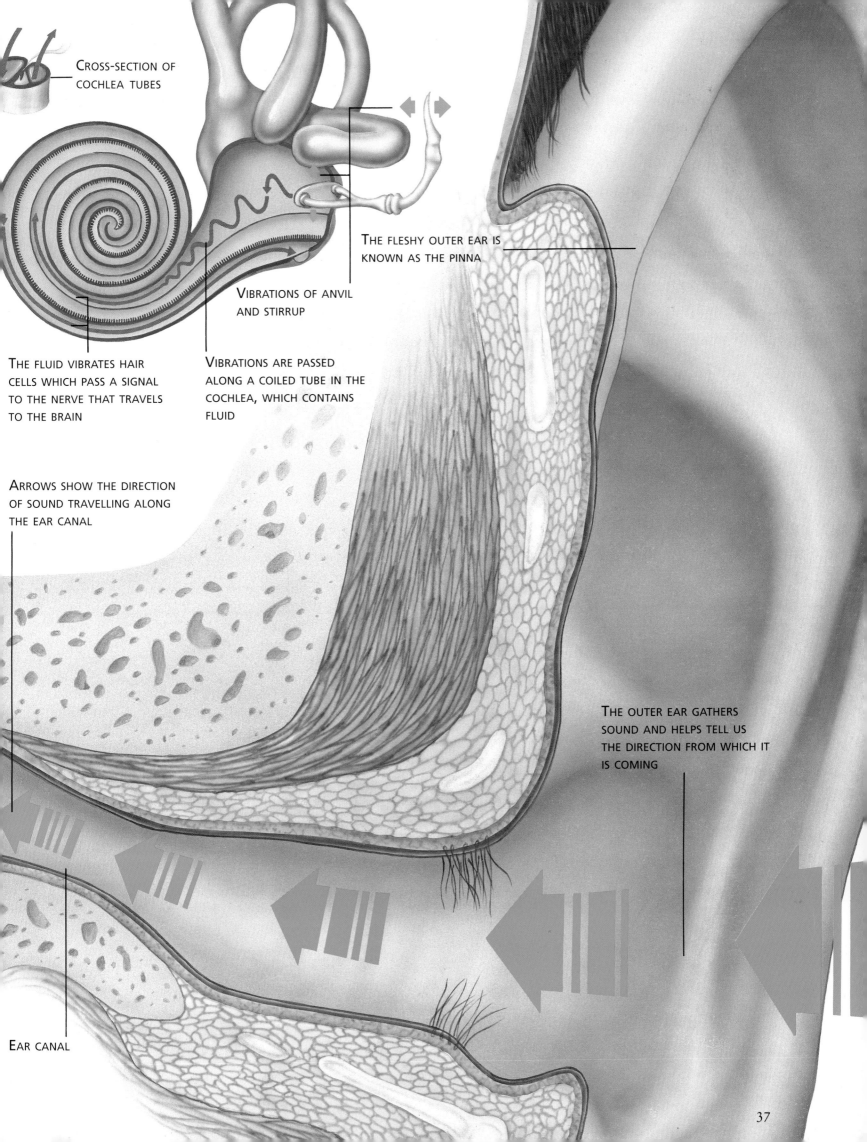

CROSS-SECTION OF
COCHLEA TUBES

THE FLESHY OUTER EAR IS
KNOWN AS THE PINNA

VIBRATIONS OF ANVIL
AND STIRRUP

THE FLUID VIBRATES HAIR
CELLS WHICH PASS A SIGNAL
TO THE NERVE THAT TRAVELS
TO THE BRAIN

VIBRATIONS ARE PASSED
ALONG A COILED TUBE IN THE
COCHLEA, WHICH CONTAINS
FLUID

ARROWS SHOW THE DIRECTION
OF SOUND TRAVELLING ALONG
THE EAR CANAL

THE OUTER EAR GATHERS
SOUND AND HELPS TELL US
THE DIRECTION FROM WHICH IT
IS COMING

EAR CANAL

Reproduction

It takes two cells for human sexual reproduction to occur: a woman's egg-cell and a man's sperm-cell. These cells have to meet and join together in order for a baby to be made. This process is called fertilization, and it normally only occurs when a couple has had sexual intercourse. When a man becomes excited his normally limp penis becomes hard and enlarged from a rush of blood. This makes him able to slide it into a woman's vagina. The penis becomes more stimulated by movements of sexual intercourse until the man has an orgasm. When this occurs a fluid called semen, which contains sperm, is released from the man's penis into the woman's vagina.

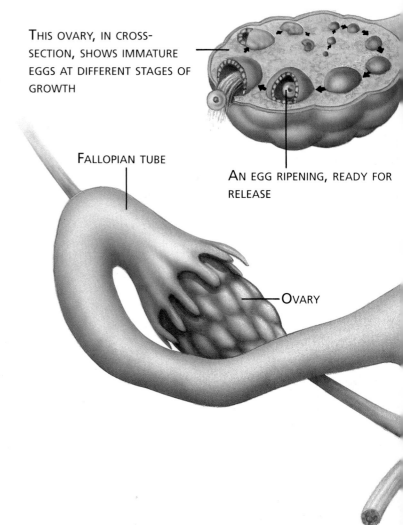

THIS OVARY, IN CROSS-SECTION, SHOWS IMMATURE EGGS AT DIFFERENT STAGES OF GROWTH

FALLOPIAN TUBE

AN EGG RIPENING, READY FOR RELEASE

OVARY

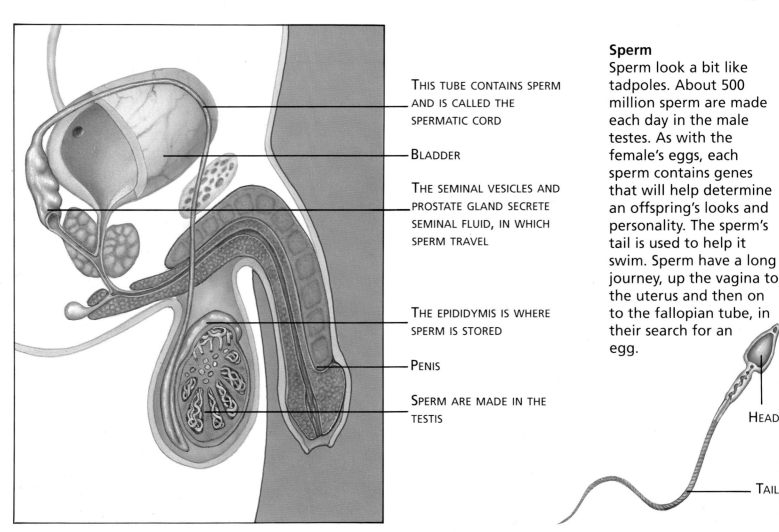

THIS TUBE CONTAINS SPERM AND IS CALLED THE SPERMATIC CORD

BLADDER

THE SEMINAL VESICLES AND PROSTATE GLAND SECRETE SEMINAL FLUID, IN WHICH SPERM TRAVEL

THE EPIDIDYMIS IS WHERE SPERM IS STORED

PENIS

SPERM ARE MADE IN THE TESTIS

Sperm
Sperm look a bit like tadpoles. About 500 million sperm are made each day in the male testes. As with the female's eggs, each sperm contains genes that will help determine an offspring's looks and personality. The sperm's tail is used to help it swim. Sperm have a long journey, up the vagina to the uterus and then on to the fallopian tube, in their search for an egg.

HEAD

TAIL

Eggs and fertilization

Women usually release one egg each month from one of their two ovaries. The egg is sent from the ovary down the fallopian tube, which is where fertilization occurs. One sperm penetrates the egg, by breaking through its outer wall. Other sperm are then prevented from entering. The sperm and egg join together to form a cell that divides, again and again, to form a clump that attaches to the uterine wall. This clump of cells soon forms an embryo, which grows into a fetus.

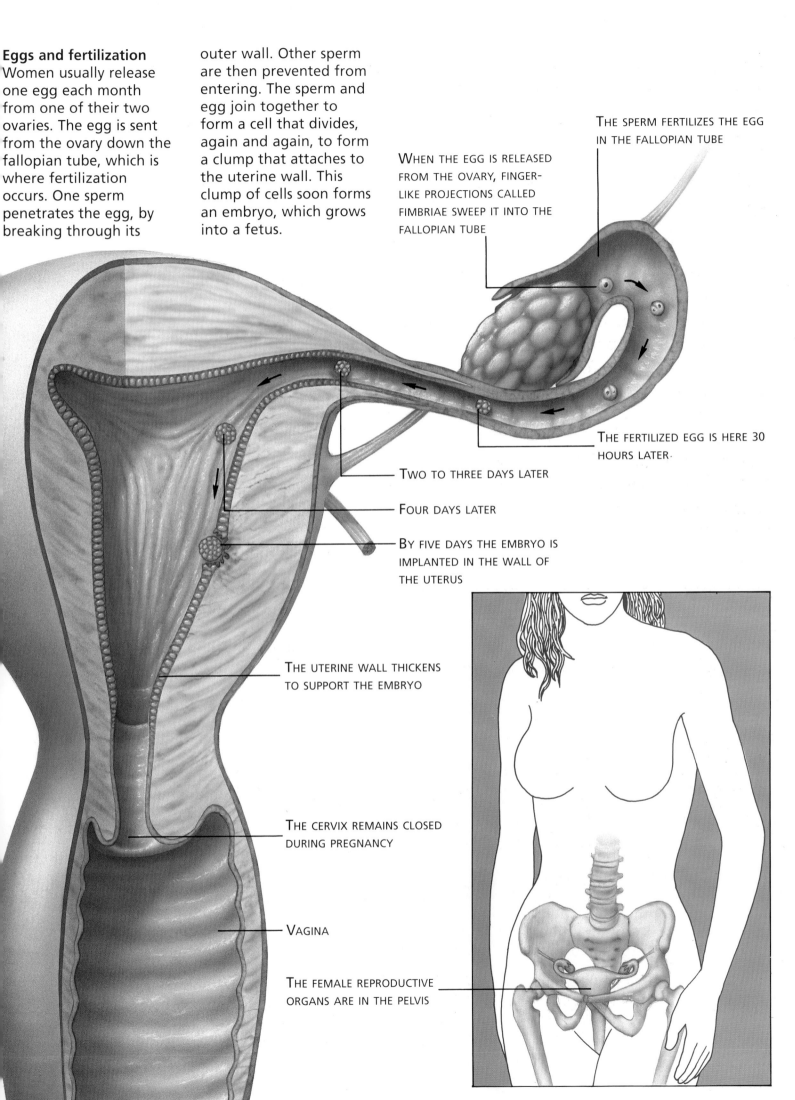

THE SPERM FERTILIZES THE EGG IN THE FALLOPIAN TUBE

WHEN THE EGG IS RELEASED FROM THE OVARY, FINGER-LIKE PROJECTIONS CALLED FIMBRIAE SWEEP IT INTO THE FALLOPIAN TUBE

THE FERTILIZED EGG IS HERE 30 HOURS LATER

TWO TO THREE DAYS LATER

FOUR DAYS LATER

BY FIVE DAYS THE EMBRYO IS IMPLANTED IN THE WALL OF THE UTERUS

THE UTERINE WALL THICKENS TO SUPPORT THE EMBRYO

THE CERVIX REMAINS CLOSED DURING PREGNANCY

VAGINA

THE FEMALE REPRODUCTIVE ORGANS ARE IN THE PELVIS

How a Baby Grows

EACH OF US begins life as a tiny, microscopic cell. In just nine months this single cell becomes a baby, fully-formed and ready to be born. First, inside the mother, the cell divides into a hollow ball of many cells. This becomes attached to the side of the mother's uterus, and grows into what we call the fetus. The head soon grows, the arms and legs appear, and the fetus begins to look like a human being. A tube, called the umbilical cord, carries the fetus's blood to and from the placenta. In the placenta the fetus's blood mixes with the mother's blood. When the baby is ready to be born, chemicals signal the mother's uterus to push the baby out. The umbilical cord is cut, leaving the new-born baby with a small scar – the belly button.

Stages of growth

To grow and survive the fetus needs nutrition and oxygen from its mother's blood. Inside the placenta there are vessels linking the mother's and fetus's blood. Waste chemicals from the fetus's blood are taken away by the mother's blood, and the mother's blood feeds the fetus. After two months the main parts of the baby's body are formed. At this stage it looks rather strange as its head seems too big for its body. At five months the toenails, fingernails, and all the main organs have formed. Even the eyelashes have appeared. By seven and a half months it looks almost like a new-born baby. It is about 15 inches long, while at birth a baby is usually 19.5 inches. If the baby were born at this earlier stage, it would still be able to survive if given special care and attention. When a baby is born early it is called premature.

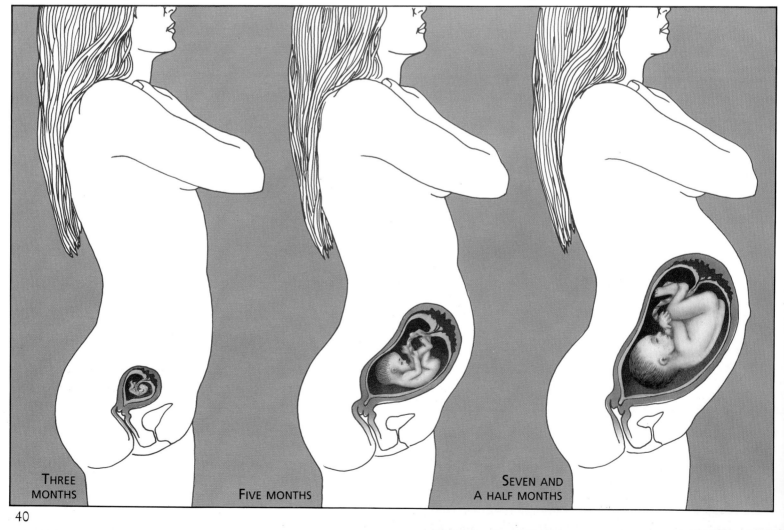

THREE MONTHS

FIVE MONTHS

SEVEN AND A HALF MONTHS

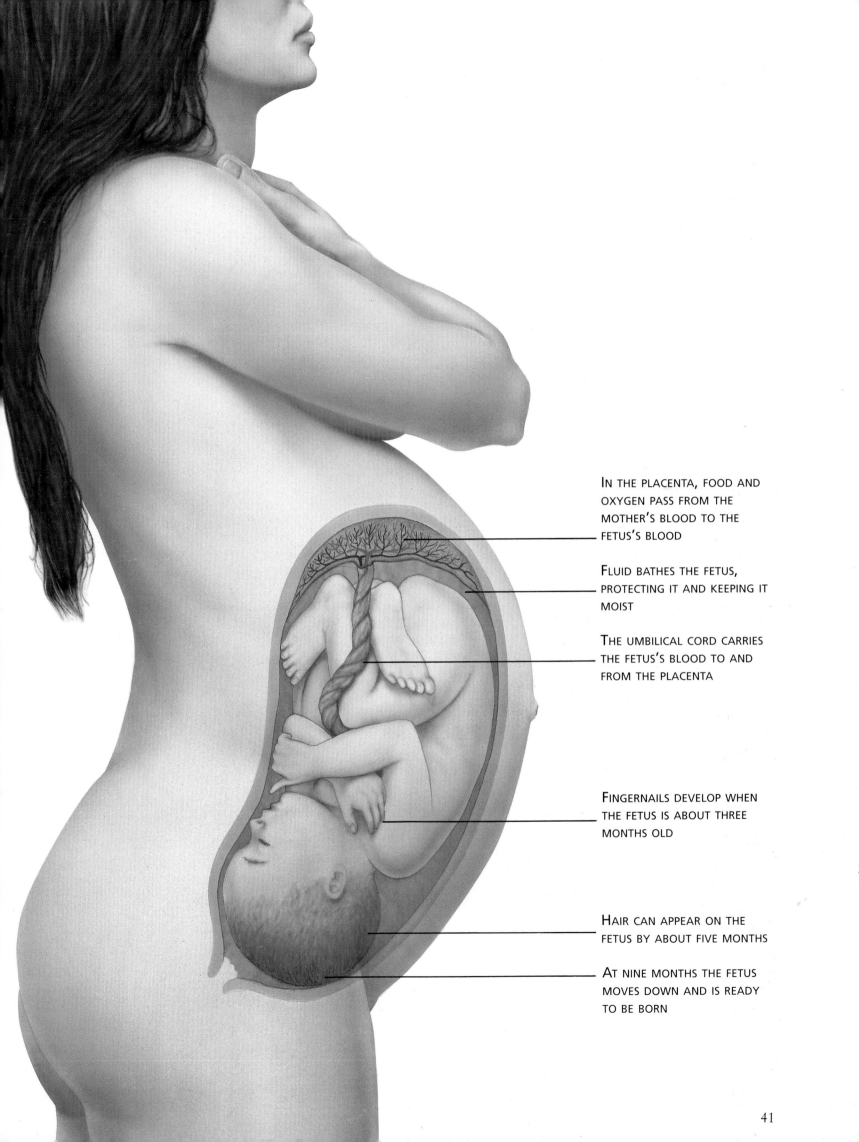

IN THE PLACENTA, FOOD AND OXYGEN PASS FROM THE MOTHER'S BLOOD TO THE FETUS'S BLOOD

FLUID BATHES THE FETUS, PROTECTING IT AND KEEPING IT MOIST

THE UMBILICAL CORD CARRIES THE FETUS'S BLOOD TO AND FROM THE PLACENTA

FINGERNAILS DEVELOP WHEN THE FETUS IS ABOUT THREE MONTHS OLD

HAIR CAN APPEAR ON THE FETUS BY ABOUT FIVE MONTHS

AT NINE MONTHS THE FETUS MOVES DOWN AND IS READY TO BE BORN

Fighting Germs

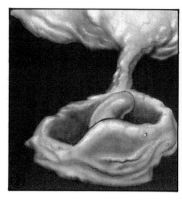

MILLIONS of germs, known as bacteria and viruses, lie on and in our body. They don't usually harm us because they cannot easily pass through our skin or the acid in our stomach. However, if they do get past these barriers an army of white cells is called in to protect us. Most white cells are contained in lymph tissue, such as the tonsils and spleen, as well as in our blood. There are several different types of white cell that make up the immune system. The most common are the polymorphs, which destroy germs. Sometimes germs have protective coatings to help them avoid capture by polymorphs. When this happens specially-shaped structures called anti-bodies are produced that lock into the germ's coating, breaking the germ apart.

Destroying a germ
The first picture (1) illustrates how a polymorph white cell works. On receiving a chemical message saying that a bacterium is invading, it moves to the area of invasion and makes part of its cell longer. This elongated part moves towards the bacteria and swallows it (2). The bacterium is actually sucked into the polymorph, surrounded

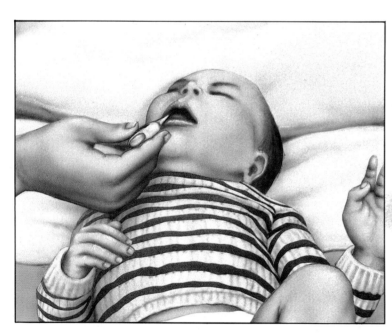

Immunization
Many diseases that were very common 40 or 50 years ago are rare in developed countries today. This is mainly because most of the people receive vaccines against these diseases. Nowadays, we are given vaccinations when we are children, either by injection or by mouth. Vaccinations put dead or weakened germs into our bodies. These germs, not harmful enough to make us very ill, cause us to produce antibodies that remain in our bodies over a long period of time and protect us from an attack by live, disease-causing germs.

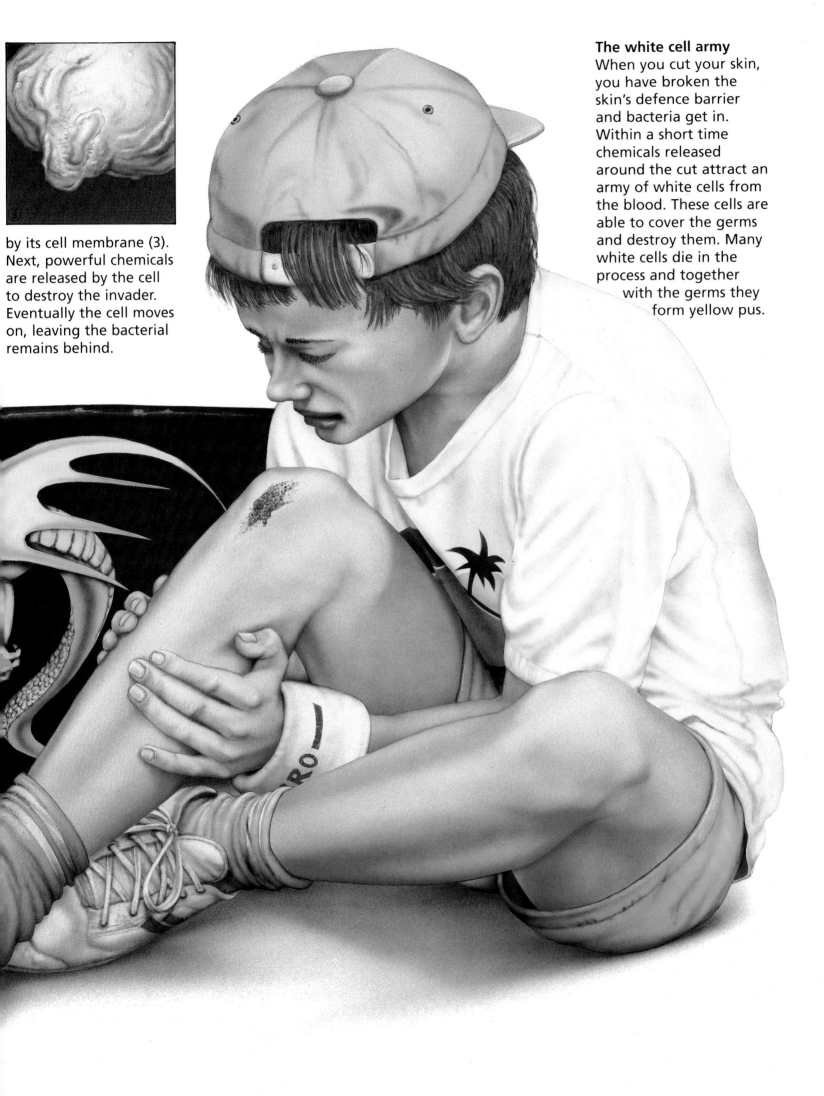

by its cell membrane (3). Next, powerful chemicals are released by the cell to destroy the invader. Eventually the cell moves on, leaving the bacterial remains behind.

The white cell army
When you cut your skin, you have broken the skin's defence barrier and bacteria get in. Within a short time chemicals released around the cut attract an army of white cells from the blood. These cells are able to cover the germs and destroy them. Many white cells die in the process and together with the germs they form yellow pus.

Spare Parts

FORTUNATELY, today many people with diseases can be helped by organ transplants. Patients with organs – such as a heart or kidney – that are badly diseased can have healthy organs surgically transplanted to replace their own. These operations rely on the goodwill of people who say their organs can be used for this purpose after they die.

Some people do not need organ transplants, but may be helped by artificial implants. For example, artificial limbs have been developed for people who have lost a leg or an arm. Surgeons can also use parts of the patient's own body to treat his or her disease. Veins from a patient's leg, for example, can be used to replace a damaged artery in their heart.

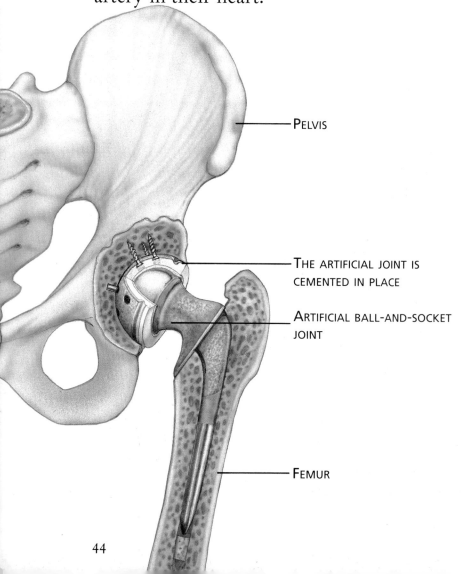

PELVIS

THE ARTIFICIAL JOINT IS CEMENTED IN PLACE

ARTIFICIAL BALL-AND-SOCKET JOINT

FEMUR

Joint replacements
One of the most common artificial replacements is of the hip joint. Hip replacements are normally given to people who have developed osteoarthritis. This is a condition caused by wear and tear on joints that happens as we get older. When it affects the hip it causes a lot of pain and difficulty in getting about. The artificial hip joint is usually made of metal and is cemented into the bone in the upper leg once the old joint has been removed.

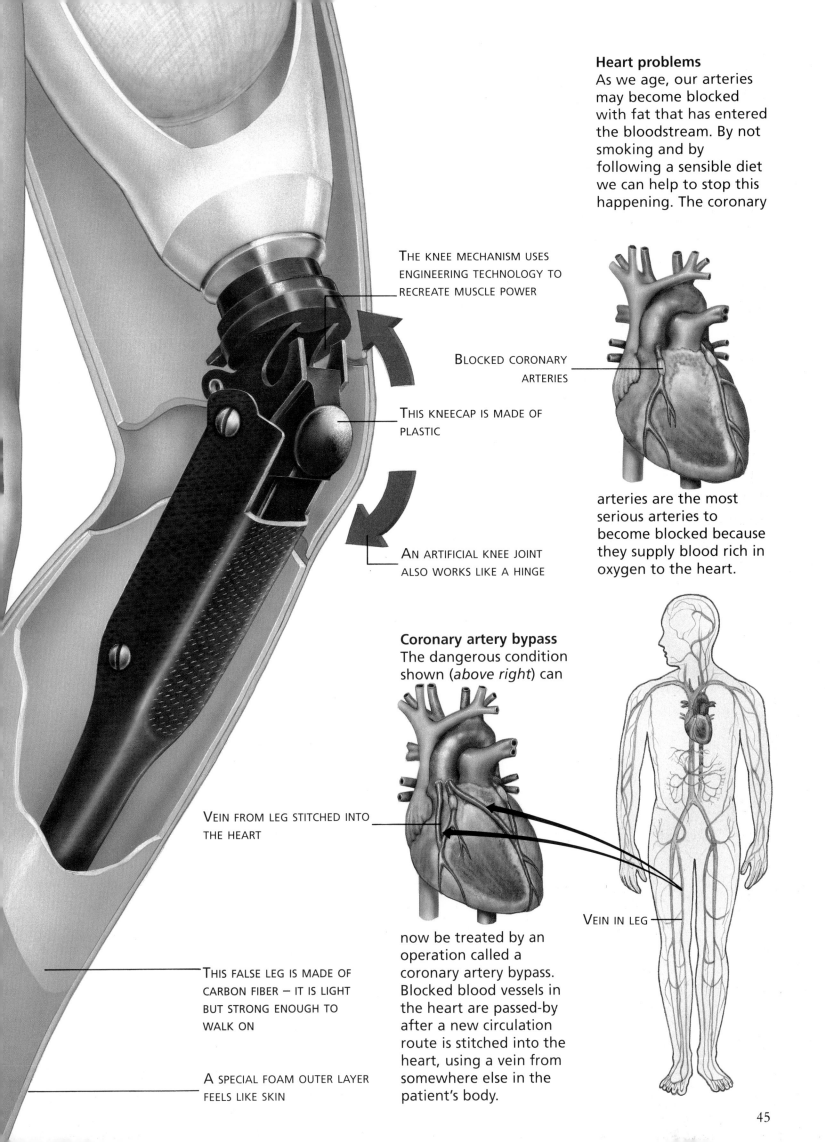

THE KNEE MECHANISM USES
ENGINEERING TECHNOLOGY TO
RECREATE MUSCLE POWER

THIS KNEECAP IS MADE OF
PLASTIC

AN ARTIFICIAL KNEE JOINT
ALSO WORKS LIKE A HINGE

VEIN FROM LEG STITCHED INTO
THE HEART

THIS FALSE LEG IS MADE OF
CARBON FIBER — IT IS LIGHT
BUT STRONG ENOUGH TO
WALK ON

A SPECIAL FOAM OUTER LAYER
FEELS LIKE SKIN

Heart problems

As we age, our arteries
may become blocked
with fat that has entered
the bloodstream. By not
smoking and by
following a sensible diet
we can help to stop this
happening. The coronary

BLOCKED CORONARY
ARTERIES

arteries are the most
serious arteries to
become blocked because
they supply blood rich in
oxygen to the heart.

Coronary artery bypass

The dangerous condition
shown (*above right*) can

now be treated by an
operation called a
coronary artery bypass.
Blocked blood vessels in
the heart are passed-by
after a new circulation
route is stitched into the
heart, using a vein from
somewhere else in the
patient's body.

VEIN IN LEG

Index